An Introduction to Syriac Studies

Gorgias Handbooks

Gorgias Handbooks provides students and scholars with reference books, textbooks and introductions to different topics or fields of study. In this series, Gorgias welcomes books that are able to communicate information, ideas and concepts effectively and concisely, with useful reference bibliographies for further study.

An Introduction to Syriac Studies

Third Edition

Sebastian P. Brock

GORGIAS PRESS

2017

Gorgias Press LLC, 954 River Road, Piscataway, NJ, 08854, USA

www.gorgiaspress.com

Copyright © 2017 by Gorgias Press LLC

2017 ܬ

ISBN 978-1-4632-0713-7   ISSN 1935-6838

Library of Congress Cataloging-in-Publication Data

A Cataloging-in-Publication Record is Available from the Library of Congress.

Printed in the United States of America

CONTENTS

PREFACE

This Introduction to Syriac Studies was originally written for a volume entitled *Horizons in Semitic Studies. Articles for the Student*, edited by J. H. Eaton, and published by the Department of Theology, University of Birmingham, in 1980. In many ways it is gratifying that, a quarter of a century later, so much has needed altering in Chapter V: several areas, for which there were no useful aids twenty-five years ago, are now reasonably well provided for—not, of course, that there is not a great deal still to do in the way of providing helpful introductory material.

As the subtitle "Articles for the Student" indicated, the original volume was primarily aimed at undergraduates who might be thinking of going on to do research. In revising the Introduction I have had more in mind graduate students, both those setting out on serious research in some area of Syriac studies, and those who are working in related fields, such as the history and literature of Late Antiquity and early Islam, and need some guidance in finding their way around less familiar, or maybe totally unfamiliar, territory. (Those to whom the identity of the various Syriac Churches is something of a mystery would find it helpful to look at the opening paragraphs of the Appendix at an early stage).

I am most grateful to a number of people: to my former colleague in the Department of Theology at the University of Birmingham, John Eaton, the editor of the original home of this Introduction; to Kristian Heal, who put the original text into electronic form on the Internet; to Dayroyo (Monk) Elie Khalifeh for his technical help in providing me with a text from which to make the revision; to George Kiraz of the Gorgias Press for accepting to publish the updated form of the Introduction; and to my many friends in the various different Syriac communities for the inspiration they provide: it is to the memory of one of these, Father Yusuf Habbi (d. 15 x 2000) of the Chaldean Church, who did so much to promote Syriac studies, both in his own country, Iraq, and elsewhere, that I should like to dedicate this second edition.

Sebastian Brock
Oxford
30 July, 2005
Commemoration of Bar ʿEbroyo

PREFACE TO THE THIRD EDITION

In this third edition a number of changes and additions have been made: the bibliographical references and other information have all been brought up to date, and in Chapter V. TOOLS, two further sections have been added, 'Online Resources for Syriac Studies', and 'Syriac Studies, Past and Present'. Chapter VI has also been slightly expanded.

Sebastian Brock
23 February, 2017
Commemoration of St Polycarp

I. WHAT IS SYRIAC?

Whether one is in, say, London, Paris, Amsterdam, Berlin, Detroit, Toronto, or Sydney, one should be able to find a church where all or part of the Liturgy on a Sunday is celebrated in Syriac. In the past one would have had to travel to the Middle East for this, but today there is a huge diaspora in Europe, the Americas, and Australia of people from the different Syriac Churches.[1] One of the first things that a visitor to such a service is likely to be told is that Syriac is a form of Aramaic, the language of Jesus in first-century Palestine, a fact of which members of all the Syriac Churches are extremely proud.

Syriac continues today as a liturgical language in current use in two Syriac Churches in particular, the Church of the East and the Syrian Orthodox Church. To a lesser extent it is also used in the Liturgy of the Maronite Church, but in recent decades Arabic has been making rapid inroads there at the expense of Syriac.

Classical Syriac, however, is by no means just a "dead" liturgical language: it is still employed as a literary language, especially among the Syrian Orthodox, and in some circles it is even spoken and taught to children (it is the normal language of communication, for example, in the Syrian Orthodox monastic school of Mar Gabriel in Tur Abdin, in southeastern Turkey, where the children may come from Arabic-, Turkish-, Kurdish-, or Turoyo (modern Syriac) -speaking backgrounds). Within the last century several European works of literature have been translated into Syriac—including Shakespeare's *Merchant of Venice* and Dickens' *Tale of Two Cities*. Numerous cultural magazines containing sections with contributions written in Classical Syriac are currently being published, both by the diaspora in Europe and elsewhere, and in the Middle East: one that started publication in 2005 is entitled *Kurkmo*, "Saffron," since it is published by the Dayro d-Kurkmo, the Saffron Monastery (Deirulzafaran), just outside Mardin in southeastern Turkey (the Syrian Orthodox bishop of Mardin, Mor[2] Filoksinos Saliba, has an MSt in Syriac Studies from Oxford

---

[1] For these, and the different terms used for them, see the Appendix.
[2] Mor (or Mar) is an honorific title used both for bishops and for saints.

1

University). Mardin itself now has a university where Syriac is taught, and in 2008 an international conference on the Syriac language was held there.

II. WHY STUDY IT?

But just as people do not learn Hebrew in order to read the Hebrew translation of Goethe's *Faust*, so no one is going to learn Syriac for the purpose of reading Dickens; nor is anyone today likely to find it useful (as St. Hilarion did, according to his biographer Jerome) for exorcizing possessed Bactrian camels. There are, however, other incentives, for there exists an extensive range of fine native Syriac literature, especially poetry, as well as of translations into Syriac from Greek and other languages, dating from the second century up to the present day. What is commonly regarded as the best of this literature, however, was written in the 300–400 years prior to the advent of Islam, and with one or two exceptions it is the literature of this "golden age" that has attracted the greatest attention among Western scholars. In recent years, however, there has been an increasing interest in the period of Late Antiquity and the transition to Islam, which has led historians to take much more interest in the Syriac sources for this period. It is worth looking at some of the areas which have claimed the particular interest of scholars.

A. BIBLICAL STUDIES

The study of Syriac has long been seen as an important adjunct to biblical studies. The first printed edition of the Syriac New Testament goes back to 1555 (the earliest European Syriac grammar dates from 1539), and the standard Syriac version of both Old and New Testaments, known as the Peshitta, features in the great Paris and London polyglot Bibles of the seventeenth century alongside the other ancient versions.

The Old Testament books were translated into Syriac directly from Hebrew, probably over a period by different people sometime in the second century AD. The fact that the translation was made from Hebrew, rather than from the Septuagint, makes it likely that at least some books will have been translated by Jews, and that in the case of any books translated by Christians, these Christians will have been converts from Judaism who still retained a knowledge of Hebrew.

It is striking that Syriac tradition has no account of the origins of its biblical versions such as we have for the Septuagint in the Letter of

Aristeas. Some books, in particular those of the Pentateuch, have certain features in common with the extant Jewish Aramaic Targumim, and it is possible that the translators of the Targumim and of these books in the Peshitta share a common Palestinian background. In the case of one book, Proverbs, there is, remarkably enough, a direct literary relationship, for the extant Targum of this book is evidently derived from the Peshitta (and not the other way round, as one might have expected).

Since the oldest Syriac translations of Old Testament books date from after the period of the stabilization of the Hebrew text in the first century AD, the Peshitta Old Testament is of less interest than the Septuagint to textual critics of the Hebrew Bible, although it does nevertheless offer number of interesting readings which feature in the apparatus of Biblia Hebraica and Biblia Hebraica Stuttgartensia.

The Peshitta Old Testament is remarkably well provided with ancient manuscripts: the oldest dated biblical manuscript in any language, of 459/60, contains the Peshitta version of Isaiah, and there is an impressive number of manuscripts dating from the sixth century.

Besides the standard version of the Old Testament, the Peshitta, there is a further translation, this time made from Greek in Alexandria around AD 615. Known as the Syrohexapla and made by Paul of Tella, this is a very literal translation of Origen's revised Septuagint text in the Hexapla, together with his critical signs (asterisks and obeli) and many marginal readings derived from the Jewish Greek translators, Aquila, Theodotion, and Symmachus. Not quite the whole of the Syrohexapla survives, but since very little of Origen's Hexapla remains in Greek the Syrohexapla is a witness of prime importance for Septuagint studies.

The only book of the so-called Apocrypha, or Deutero-Canonical literature, to be translated from Hebrew is Ben Sira (Ecclesiasticus); for all the remaining books the Syriac translators used the Greek text as their basis.

It is interesting to see that in the history of translation into Syriac (whether of biblical or of non-biblical texts) there is a continuous move away from the free to the very literal, a process which reaches its climax in the seventh century.

There are several versions of the Syriac New Testament; of these, the oldest is probably a harmony of the Four Gospels, the Diatessaron associated with the name of Tatian (he appears occasionally to have used some other sources as well). This work, whose original language, Syriac or Greek, and whose relationship to the Western Diatessaron tradition, remains uncertain, dates from the second half of the second century AD. It enjoyed wide popularity in the early Syriac Church, but was eventually suppressed in the early fifth century; as a result, no complete Syriac text of it survives: the nearest we have is Ephrem's Commentary on it, the Syriac original of which only came to light just over half a century ago. Although little is known of its original form, the influence of the Diatessaron was very widespread and we have medieval adaptations in Persian and Arabic, as well as in medieval German, Dutch, Italian, and English. Some of its distinctive readings have retained an after-life in the Syriac liturgical tradition.

The earliest Syriac Gospel text that survives is known as the Old Syriac, and is preserved, not quite complete, in two very old manuscripts, the Curetonian (in the British Library), and the Sinaiticus (at the monastery of St. Catherine on Mt. Sinai), to these two manuscripts some twenty folios of a third Old Syriac Gospel manuscript can now be added, also at St Catherine's Monastery and, like the Sinaiticus, a palimpsest. Textually, the Old Syriac Gospel text is of very great interest, exhibiting a number of "Western" readings. Along with the Old Latin it is the oldest surviving translation of the Greek Gospels. It is likely that the Old Syriac once covered the whole Syriac New Testament Canon (which excludes Revelation, 2 Peter, 2 and 3 John, and Jude), but only quotations from books other than the Gospels survive.

The standard New Testament version, the Peshitta, is a revision of the Old Syriac, completed probably around the beginning of the early fifth century. The work of revision has sometimes been associated with the name of Rabbula, bishop of Edessa (411–36), but this now seems unlikely. The distribution of the revised text was evidently very effective since Peshitta manuscripts (of which several go back to the late fifth century) show remarkably little variation among themselves: the oldest Peshitta Gospel manuscript was written in Edessa in 510, and constitutes the earliest dated Gospel manuscript in any language. Several other Peshitta manuscripts that are undated probably go back even earlier, to the late fifth century.

In the early sixth century the Peshitta was brought yet further into line with the Greek original under the auspices of the great Syrian Orthodox theologian Philoxenus, bishop of Mabbug, who had found certain passages in the Peshitta (notably Matt. 1:1, 1:18; Heb. 5:7 and 10:5) too free and susceptible of a "Nestorian" interpretation. His version, known as the Philoxenian (although it was a certain chorepiscopus Polycarp who actually did the work, completing it in 507/8) does not survive in its original form, but a century later it served as a basis for yet another revision, made by Thomas of Harkel in Alexandria, about 615. Thomas's work, known as the Harklean, survives in a number of manuscripts (some of the seventh and eighth centuries) and, along with Paul of Tella's contemporary Syrohexapla, it represents the peak of sophistication in the technique of literal translation: every detail of the Greek original is reflected—which greatly eases the work of the modern textual critic who is interested in reconstructing the underlying Greek text!

An excellent survey of the Syriac New Testament versions is to be found in chapter one of B. M. Metzger's *The Early Versions of the New Testament* (Oxford, 1977), while for the Old Testament there is M. Weitzman's valuable *The Syriac Version of the Old Testament. An Introduction* (Cambridge, 1999). An overview, which also covers something of the reception history of the Syriac Bible as well, can be found in my *The Bible in the Syriac Tradition* (2nd edition, Piscataway NJ, 2006). (For further details, see Chapter V, D)

B. PATRISTIC STUDIES

A very large number of the works of the Church Fathers was translated into Syriac, sometimes more than once. The earliest to survive are some of Eusebius' works, including the *Theophania*, largely lost in its Greek original; all these happen to be preserved in fifth century manuscripts. The process of translating Greek texts continued apace until the end of the seventh century, by which time the Arab invasions had largely cut off the Syriac-speaking churches from close contact with Greek world of what was left of the Byzantine Empire.

Syriac translations of the Greek Church Fathers are of twofold interest. In the case of works where the Greek originals survive, the Syriac translation not only usually antedates the earliest Greek manuscript by many centuries, but is itself preserved in manuscripts of great antiquity (sixth-century manuscripts are not uncommon).

Even more important are the Syriac translations of works whose Greek originals are lost: besides Eusebius' *Theophania*, just mentioned, these include treatises attributed to Hippolytus and Gregory Thaumaturgus, Athanasius' *Festal Letters*, Theodore of Mopsuestia's *Catechetical Homilies* and *Commentary on John*, Cyril of Alexandria's *Commentary on Luke*, and various works by Evagrius Ponticus. Syriac also preserves in translation the writings of several Greek anti-Chalcedonian theologians whose works, having been suppressed in their Greek form, would otherwise have been totally lost to us; most notable in this category are the voluminous works of Severus, patriarch of Antioch from 512 until 518, when he had to flee to Egypt for the next twenty years of his life.

A list of the main longer Patristic texts translated into Greek is given in the bibliography section of T. Muraoka's *A Basic Syriac Grammar* (2nd ed., Wiesbaden, 2005), pp. 153–5. M. Geerhard's *Clavis Patrum Graecorum* (Turnhout, 1974–83; Supplement, 1998) indicates if a Syriac translation exists for any particular work, and based on this are the convenient listings by D. Gonnet in his contribution to *Les Pères grecs dans la tradition syriaque* (Études syriaques 4; Paris, 1907), 195-212.

C. LITURGICAL STUDIES

For anyone who has an interest in the history of liturgy Syriac has great riches to offer. It was the general area of Syria/Palestine that proved the most creative and fertile in this field for early Christianity, and it was from here that the rich Byzantine liturgies of St. John Chrysostom, St. Basil, and St. James ultimately derived; here too, more than anywhere else, did liturgical poetry, in both Greek and Syriac, flourish. The East Syriac Liturgy of St. Addai and St. Mari happens to be the oldest liturgy still in regular use, while West Syriac tradition has produced an astonishing abundance of anaphoras: over 70 come down to us, and of these a dozen or so are still commonly employed.

Of particular importance to the student of comparative liturgy is the early Syrian baptismal rite, consisting of an anointing followed by immersion in water, a sequence evidently modelled on the Jewish initiation rite of circumcision and proselyte baptism. Only around AD 400 was a post-baptismal anointing introduced, thus gradually bringing Antiochene baptismal practice into line with that of other areas.

Syriac is exceptional in that is the transmitter of liturgical texts of four different Church traditions, the Church of the East, the Syrian Orthodox and the Maronite Churches, and the Chalcedonian Orthodox Patriarchate of Antioch, for which Syriac remained as one of its three liturgical languages (the others being Greek and Arabic) until the mid seventeenth century. Largely still unexplored Syriac manuscripts provide evidence for the remarkable change of liturgical rite, from Antiochene to Constantinopolitan, which took place within the Chalcedonian Patriarchate of Antioch over the course of the tenth to twelfth century, involving translations from Greek into Syriac of all the main liturgical books in use in Constantinople at the time.

The critical study of the contents of the many liturgical books in use in the various Syriac Churches is still very much in its infancy. A general introduction to the West Syriac tradition is available in B. Varghese's *West Syrian Liturgical Theology* (Aldershot, 2004). Mention should also be made of the useful bibliographical guide provided by A. Baumstark (one of the pioneers in the study of Syriac liturgy) in the appendix to his fascinating book, *Comparative Liturgy* (English translation: London, 1958), and of the two specialized bibliographies, by J. M. Sauget, *Bibliographie des liturgies orientales 1900–60* (Rome, 1962), and by P. Yousif, *A Classified Bibliography on the East Syrian Liturgy* (Rome, 1990).

D. EARLY SYRIAC CHRISTIANITY

So far we have only considered the interest of Syriac as an appendage to larger fields of study, but Syriac literature is also of value in its own right, and here we may select two particular aspects, early Syriac literature as the sole surviving representative of an indigenous Semitic Christianity, and religious poetry, the genre in which Syriac writers best excelled.

The earliest major authors whose names we know, Aphrahat and Ephrem, both of the fourth century, are little affected by Greek culture and they offer us a largely unhellenized form of Christianity that is deeply biblical in character and quite different in many respects from the Christianity of the Greek- and Latin-speaking world of the Mediterranean littoral. From the fifth to seventh century, however, Syriac-speaking Christianity underwent a process of ever increasing hellenization, with the result that no subsequent writers entirely escape from the influence of Greek culture in some form or other. Accordingly, it is primarily to these two early writers, Aphrahat and Ephrem, that we must turn in order to examine this phenomenon. This specific aspect of the earliest Syriac literature has been curiously neglected, despite its potential interest for the study of primitive Christianity as a whole, for which its relevance could be said to be much the same as that of Rabbinic literature for New Testament studies.

The fact that the earliest Syriac writers are largely "uncontaminated" by Greek—and hence European—culture also makes this literature of particular interest to modern Asian and African Churches which, quite apart from an understandable desire to be rid of Christianity's various European cultural trappings, find themselves more at home with Semitic than with Greek thought patterns.

An excellent and sympathetic introduction to this world of typology and symbolic theology will be found in R. Murray's *Symbols of Church and Kingdom* (Cambridge, 1975; new edition, Piscataway NJ, 2004). There is also a good presentation in what might seem an unlikely place, C. Buck's *Paradise and Paradigm. Key Symbols in Persian Christianity and the Baha'i Faith* (Albany, 1999).

A further particularly interesting feature of early Syriac Christianity is the early ascetic tradition and the development of a form of "proto-monasticism," along very different lines from the more familiar forms that developed in Egypt. An excellent introduction to this is given by S. H. Griffith, "Asceticism in the Church of Syria. The hermeneutics of early Syrian monasticism," in V. L. Wimbush and R. Valantasis (eds.), *Asceticism* (New York, 1995).

E. SYRIAC POETRY

Syriac literature has produced (and indeed still continues to produce) a very large number of poets, but one in particular among them towers in stature as a poet of real originality and spiritual insight, Ephrem of Nisibis, who died in 373 at Edessa; his *madrashe*, or hymns, can justly take a place among the great religious poetry of the world—despite the derogatory judgment of one or two eminent Syriac scholars of the late nineteenth and early twentieth century. Ephrem's is an allusive lyrical poetry filled with paradox and wonder, and making highly imaginative use of typological exegesis. His intricate theory of symbolism has been described as an anticipation of the basic philosophical position of Paul Ricoeur. It is unfortunate that there is still no complete English translation of his poetry.[3]

Syriac poetic form falls into two main categories, stanzaic and non-stanzaic verse; the former is known under the general title of *madrasha*, the latter under that of *memra*. *Madrashe* were certainly sung, and the titles of the melodies (called *qale*) are preserved, but not the music itself. Each stanza was picked up by a refrain, and Ephrem (whose genuine writings show a great tenderness and concern for women) was noted for having had his refrains sung by female choirs.

Syriac verse form is based on syllable count (and not on length, or stress). Each *madrasha* will be based on a particular syllabic pattern built up of smaller syllabic groupings. Ephrem employs some fifty different stanza

---

[3] The collection of *madrashe* on the Nativity and on Virginity, and those against the Emperor Julian, are translated by K. E. McVey, *Ephrem the Syrian. Hymns* (New York, 1989); the *madrashe* on Paradise are available in my *St Ephrem the Syrian, Hymns on Paradise* (Crestwood, 1990), and the large collection *On Faith* is now translated by J.T. Wickes, *St Ephrem the Syrian. The Hymns on Faith* (Washington DC, 2015). A selection of 24 poems can be found in my *The Harp of the Spirit. Poems of Saint Ephrem the Syrian* (3rd edn, Aquila Books, Cambridge UK, 2013), and an introduction to his world view in *The Luminous Eye. The Spiritual World View of St Ephrem the Syrian* (Kalamazoo, 1992).

patterns, and these can range from the very simple (e.g., four lines of four syllables each) to the extremely complex.

The *memra* was suited for narrative or moralising verse, and was the vehicle for the distinctively Syriac genre of verse homily. *Memre* were probably recited, rather than sung, and they consist of isosyllabic couplets. In any particular *memra* the couplets may consist of 5+5, 6+6, 7+7, or 12+12 syllables (in the 12+12 syllable pattern there is always a caesura, after the fourth and eighth syllable). The 5+5 syllable pattern is traditionally associated with the name of Balai (fifth century), the 7+7 with that of Ephrem, and the 12+12 with that of Jacob of Serugh (died 521).

Undoubtedly the best practitioner of the *madrasha* form was Ephrem, but there are some fine compositions by other later writers too, among which a small group of short poems by Simeon the Potter (fifth/sixth century) deserves to be singled out. The *memra* form is already found in one of the earliest surviving examples of Syriac poetry, the famous "Hymn of the Soul," preserved in the *Acts of Thomas* (6+6 syllables). In the case of Ephrem the demarcation between genuine and non-genuine is particularly hard to make where *memre* in the 7+7 syllable metre are concerned, since this was known by his name.

Notable later poets who made extensive use of the *memra* are the East Syriac Narsai, head of the famous theological school at Nisibis (late fifth century), the West Syriac Jacob of Serugh, and the three Isaacs (all of the fifth/sixth century). Jacob's verse homilies, in particular, include many beautiful explorations of biblical passages, bringing out their spiritual meaning. There are also a number of wonderfully imaginative retellings of biblical episodes in verse whose authors are completely unknown. In one of the poems on Genesis 22, it is Sarah—who is never once mentioned in the biblical text of the chapter—who turns out as the real heroine of the episode, having been tested, not once, like her husband, but twice!

According to the fifth-century church historian Sozomen, it was Harmonius, the son of Bardaisan "the philosopher of the Aramaeans," who being "deeply versed in Greek learning, was the first to subdue Syriac, his native tongue, to metres and laws." Since Bardaisan died in 222, his son Harmonius (if he is not entirely fictional) would have been active in the early third century. An examination of the actual evidence, however, indicates that the implication that Syriac verse form was based on Greek metre is totally incorrect. Evidently we are dealing with an example of Greek chauvinism, which preferred to see anything good in barbarian Syriac culture—such as Ephrem's poetry, some of it already translated into Greek by Sozomen's day—as ultimately derivative from Greek civilization. As a matter of fact it is more likely that there was influence the other way round, and that the Syriac *madrasha* provided the inspiration for the Byzantine syllabic hymn form known as the *kontakion*, developed in the fifth and sixth centuries. Most of the best Greek hymnographers happen to come from Syria or Palestine, and the greatest exponent of the *kontakion*, Romanos, originated in bilingual Homs in Syria, where he could well have heard Ephrem's *madrashe* regularly sung in church. In any case it is known from explicit statements by Theodore of Mopsuestia (died 428) and others that Syriac religious poetry was translated into Greek for use among Greek-speaking congregations.

F. SYRIAC AS A BRIDGE CULTURE

The very large number of translations into, and out of, Syriac over the course of the centuries, right up to the present day, is indicative of the numerous contacts with neighbouring languages and cultures. Syriac happens to be have the earliest surviving Middle Eastern translation of the delightful Indian animal tales, usually known under the title of Kalilah and Dimnah. This Syriac version, in fact the first of three, was made in the sixth century from a lost Middle Persian translation that was much later to be the source of the Arabic version which ultimately reached Western Europe in the seventeenth century.

Many people will be aware that a knowledge of Greek philosophy reached the medieval West by way of Arabic, travelling through Muslim Spain. What is not so widely realized is that Greek philosophy, medicine, and science did not at first reach the Arab world direct, but rather by way of Syriac. Syriac translations of the works of Aristotle and others go back to the early sixth century, and it was chiefly through the work of Syriac Christians working at Baghdad, the Abbasid capital, in the late eighth and ninth century that this process of transmission, the so-called 'Translation Movement', actually took place. Among the most famous of these translators was Hunain ibn Ishaq (died 873) who gave an interesting account of how he went about his work: having collected together the best and oldest Greek manuscripts he could find, he translated from Greek into Syriac and only then from Syriac into Arabic. The reason for this at first sight rather cumbersome procedure was that Hunain had behind him half a millennium's accumulated experience of translating technical Greek texts into Syriac, whereas for Arabic there existed no such tradition and so this meant that translation from Indo-European Greek into Semitic Arabic was most easily achieved by way of another Semitic language, Syriac. Thus it comes about that a knowledge of Syriac is essential as a background to the study of Aristotelian philosophy among the Arabs.

Thanks to the work of these translators both Arabic and Syriac preserve a number of Greek philosophical and medical works which would otherwise have been entirely lost, seeing that no Greek manuscripts of them survive. Among such works, which come down to us only in Syriac, are Nicholas of Damascus' compendium of Aristotelian philosophy, Alexander of Aphrodisias' On the Universe, a dialogue on the soul between Socrates and Erostrophos, some sayings of a lady Pythagorean philosopher called Theano, and Galen's commentary on Hippocrates' *Epidemiai* (the last only partly known in Greek and Arabic)—to name but a selection.

It was, however, not only into Arabic that translations from Syriac were made: by the end of the first millennium AD works in Syriac had found their way into languages as diverse as Greek, Armenian, Georgian, Middle Persian, Sogdian, Coptic, and Ethiopic. Among those translated into Greek was the influential Apocalypse of Methodius (late seventh century) which reached the medieval Latin West by way of a Greek translation from the Syriac original. About a century or so later a collection of discourses on the spiritual life by Isaac of Nineveh (Isaac the Syrian) was translated into Greek at the Monastery of St Sabbas, south of Jerusalem; in due course these were translated into Latin and Slavonic languages where, for example, Isaac's teaching can be found reflected in the words of Father Zosima in Dostoievsky's *The Brothers Karamazov*.

Sometimes this traffic could even be two-way, as happened dramatically with some of the Aesop literature: the Greek life of Aesop, on the one hand, contains a section taken from the Story of Ahiqar, an old Aramaic tale going back to the sixth or even seventh century BC; a collection of Aesopic fables, on the other hand, was translated into Syriac (and attributed to Josephus), only to find its way back into Greek at the end of the eleventh century AD masquerading under the name of Syntipas!

Because Syriac culture lay geographically between the Byzantine and Islamic worlds this has meant that the extensive Syriac chronicle tradition contains much that is of direct relevance to Byzantine and Islamic history, and there is a great deal of valuable source material lying there which is only beginning now to be properly tapped. The considerable number of relevant Syriac sources of interest for early Islamic history is helpfully surveyed by Robrt Hoyland in his *Seeing Islam as Others saw it: A Survey and Evaluation of Christian, Jewish and Zoroastrian Writings on early Islam* (Princeton, 1997). Several further titles of relevance here will be found in chapter V, under F and G.

III. THE SCOPE OF SYRIAC LITERATURE

Considered historically, Syriac literature can conveniently be divided up into three distinctive periods: (1) the golden age of Syriac literature, up to the seventh century; (2) the Arab period until about 1300; and (3) the period from about 1300 to the present day.

The first is the period which produced the most creative writers, and it is to this that we shall return shortly. The second period, which came to an end at about the time of the conversion of the Mongols to Islam, was essentially one of consolidation and compilation: as in the Byzantine world, this period saw the birth of an encyclopaedic type of literature, witnessing, right at its close, the appearance of the greatest of all Syriac polymaths, Gregory Abu'l Faraj, better known as Bar ʿEbroyo/Barhebraeus (died 1286). Gregory wrote on every aspect of human knowledge of his time, and it is not for nothing that he has been compared to his western contemporary Thomas Aquinas (who died slightly earlier, in 1274).

The opening of the third period was a bleak one for all Christian communities in the Middle East, but the lamp of Syriac learning and literature never died out entirely, and there has been a continuous stream of writers, right up to the present day, who have employed classical Syriac as their main literary language. In the seventeenth century we also find the earliest flowering of Modern Syriac literature, in the form of poetry from the Alqosh school (northern Iraq); it was only in the nineteenth century, however, with the establishment of a Syriac printing press at Urmia (northwestern Iran), that a written literature in Modern Syriac really got going. (Among the English works, which the American mission at Urmia translated into Modern Syriac, was Bunyan's *Pilgrim's Progress*). In the last fifty years of so there has been a renewed interest in both Classical and vernacular Syriac writing, not only in the Middle East, but also among the large emigré communities in Europe, the Americas, and Australia. A considerable boost to this has been provided by developments in computer technology and the new possibilities for publishing in Syriac script.

Syriac literature of the golden age (third to seventh centuries) emerges from anonymity (apart from Bardaisan) with the appearance of two great writers in the fourth century: Aphrahat, the author of twenty-three "Demonstrations" covering a variety of religious topics, and often touching on Jewish-Christian relations, and Ephrem, whom we have already met, undoubtedly the finest of all Syriac poets. But besides being an outstanding poet, Ephrem also wrote a number of prose commentaries on certain books of the Bible, among which his commentaries on Genesis and Exodus show an intriguing familiarity with Jewish exegetical traditions. His prose refutations of Marcion, Bardaisan, and Mani constitute an important (if frustrating) source of information on the teaching of these three "heresiarchs."

The fifth and sixth centuries witnessed a remarkable hellenization of much Syriac literature, both in style and in thought patterns, although poetry remained less affected by such influence. Among the several notable poets of this era, both Jacob of Serugh (as a pupil) and Narsai (as a teacher) were associated with the famous Persian School at Edessa, which, after its closure by the emperor Zeno in 489, moved across the border to Nisibis, safe within the confines of the Persian Empire. The history of this important and influential school, which had Narsai as its director for the last decades of the fifth century, has been the subject of a number of monographs, the most detailed being that by the great Estonian Syriac scholar, Arthur Vööbus, though there now a more critical approach, especially towards the School in Edessa, has been taken by Adam Becker, in his *Fear of God and and the Beginning of Wisdom: the School of Nisibis and the Development of Scholastic Culture in Late Antique Mesopotamia* (Philadelphia, 2006).

Since Syriac literature has largely been handed down in monasteries it is not surprising that much of it is specifically Christian in character. From the strictly theological literature two authors stand out for their originality of thought (and, in the case of the first, his style): Philoxenus of Mabbug (died 523) in the Syrian Orthodox tradition, and Babai (died 628) in that of the Church of the East. Characteristically, both men also wrote treatises on the spiritual life, a topic on which there exist many very fine works in Syriac. Best known, but only one among many Syrian mystics, is Isaac of Nineveh (late seventh century), whose writings still remain today favourite reading among the monks of Mount Athos, while in Egypt their inspiration lies behind the contemporary monastic revival in the Coptic Orthodox Church. What influence the Syriac mystics had on early Sufism is a question which still requires proper investigation.[4]

---

[4] An interesting beginning has been made by an Orthodox monk in Finland, Fr. Serafim Seppälä, in his doctoral dissertation, now published as *"In speechless ecstasy"*

Biblical exegesis is another prominent genre, with important representatives in both East and West Syriac tradition. Over the course of time commentaries on biblical books became more and more encyclopaedic and derivative in character, each writer drawing extensively from the work of his predecessors. Excellent representatives of the two theological traditions are the East Syriac Isho'dad of Merv (ninth century) and the West Syriac Dionysius bar Salibi (died 1171), both of whom have left behind them commentaries on the entire Bible. Comparison of their two works and of their sources will show that, despite theological differences, there was a good deal of mutual interaction as far as the history of exegesis is concerned. Through an Arabic adaptation of the East Syriac commentary tradition by Ibn al-Tayyib (died 1043), the contents of this exegetical tradition eventually reached Ethiopia, where they still form the basis of traditional biblical study. A few biblical commentators show a remarkable critical insight, perhaps none more so than the learned Jacob of Edessa; besides numerous penetrating "scholia" on difficult biblical passages, there survives his commentary on the six days of creation (the *Hexaemeron*) which in places takes on more the form of a scientific treatise.

An ever popular genre—and one of considerable interest from the point of view of social history—is hagiography. Some pieces of Syriac origin, such as the life of Alexis "the Man of God," were soon translated into Greek and Latin, and so came to enjoy a great vogue in the medieval West. A particularly fascinating collection of lives are those of the Persian martyrs, dating from the fourth to the seventh centuries,[5] throughout which period the Church of the East suffered intermittent persecution from the Sasanid authorities, normally at the prompting of the Zoroastrian clergy.

Hagiography is often intimately connected with local monastic history. In the early Syriac life of Symeon the Stylite we can observe the tensions between this amazing athlete of the ascetic life and the monastic community to which he belonged. How such tensions came to be resolved in the course of time can be seen from the sixth-century *Lives of the Oriental Saints*, by the Syrian Orthodox Church historian John of Ephesus.[6] Among

---

Expression and Interpretation of Mystical Experience in Classical Syriac and Sufi Literature (Helsinki, 2002).

[5] Some examples of these in translation can be found in S. P. Brock and S. A. Harvey, *Holy Women of the Syrian Orient* (Berkeley, 1987).

[6] This is a work well studied by S. A. Harvey in her *Asceticism and Society in Crisis. John of Ephesus and the Lives of Eastern Saints* (Berkeley, 1990).

East Syriac writers, Thomas of Marga's *Book of Monastic Superiors* shows how vigorous—and varied—monastic life continued to be under early Arab rule.

Insights into the daily life and problems of ecclesiastics in positions both high and low are provided by the correspondence of various bishops, including two East Syriac patriarchs, Isho'yab III in the seventh, and Timothy I in the late eighth to early ninth, century. From the latter we learn, for example, that in his day the best Syriac manuscripts containing works by Greek writers were to be found in the library of the Syrian Orthodox monastery of Mar Mattai (still functioning today in northern Iraq), and he describes how he has to resort to underhand tactics in order to borrow them for copying.

But by no means all Syriac literature is religious in character. Of particular importance for the historian are the various chronicles, of which there is a long line culminating in those of Michael the Syrian and Barhebraeus, both valuable sources for the history of the Crusades. Among the earliest works of this sort is the delightfully naïve *Chronicle of Joshua the Stylite*, a source from which (to use Peter Brown's words) "we can learn more about what it was like to live (and to starve) on the streets of an ancient city, than we can ever know about the Rome of Cicero."

Mention has already been made of Syriac philosophical and scientific literature. Although much of this was either translated from, or primarily based on, Greek works, the late Roman and early Arab period witnessed a number of scholars, such as Sergius of Resh'aina (died 536), Jacob of Edessa (died 708), George bishop of the Arabs (died 724), and Moshe bar Kepha (died 903), who wrote with considerable learning and originality on secular as well as on religious topics.

Commentaries on, and introductions to, Aristotle's logical works, constituting the *Organon*, take an important place among such writings.[7] It is interesting to observe how little effect the Arab invasions had on Syriac culture of the seventh century; the many important scholars of this century also include among them a remarkable astronomer, Severus of Sebokht, only a few of whose writings have yet been published. On a less exalted level there are works in Syriac on alchemy, the interpretation of dreams, astrology, and various forms of divination.

---

[7] A summary guide to these can be found in my 'The Syriac Commentary tradition', reprinted as Chapter XIII of *From Ephrem to Romanos* (Aldershot, 1999). Especially important is the collection of articles by H. Hugonnard-Roche, listed in Chapter V H, below.

There also survives a certain amount of essentially popular literature in Syriac, such as the animal tales of Indian origin, Kalilah and Dimnah (mentioned earlier, better known under the name of Bidpai to seventeenth-century European writers like La Fontaine). This work exists in Syriac in three different translations, the earliest made from Middle Persian in the sixth century, the other two from Arabic, were made in the ninth and nineteenth century.

Of native Syriac origin are the lively contest and dialogue poems, with two protagonists speaking in alternate verses. Usually these have been given a thin liturgical veneer, and it is this which has ensured their survival. This is actually a genre which goes back to ancient Mesopotamia, from where we have examples in both Sumerian and Akkadian; subsequently it was to be taken up by the Arabs (known as the *munazara*), and, perhaps by way of Spain, by medieval Spanish and Provencal jongleurs. In the Middle East the genre has continued right up to the present day in several different languages. In Syriac the genre was first adapted by Ephrem who has three three lively poems where Death and Satan dispute over which of the two has the greatest influence over human beings. Later Syriac precedence disputes have protagonists such as Earth and Heaven, the Months of the Year, Wheat and Gold, the Vine and the Cedar, and so on. The majority of the Syriac dialogue poems, however, concern biblical characters such as Abel and Cain, Abraham and Isaac, Mary and the Angel, Mary and Joseph, or the sword-wielding Cherub of Genesis 3:24 and the Repentant Thief at the gate of Paradise. Combining insight, humour, and teaching, these delightful poems deserve to be revived and perhaps be adapted for different modern contexts.

Several important areas of Syriac literature have been passed over in silence—the extensive apocryphal literature, and the canonical and legal texts,[8] to name but a couple—but sufficient has by now been said to give some idea of the variety to be found within the confines of Syriac literature, and it is time to turn to look at the place of Syriac among the various Aramaic dialects, and then to survey some of the more important "tools of the trade."

---

[8] One legal text, however, should not go without any mention: this is the "Syro-Roman Law Book" of the late fifth century, which survives in Syriac translation: this work, of very great importance for the study of Late Antique society, has now been magnificently re-edited, with German translation and commentary, by W. Selb and H. Kaufhold, *Das syrisch-römische Rechtsbuch*, I–III (Österreichische Akademie der Wissenschaften, Vienna, 2002.

IV. THE PLACE OF SYRIAC AMONG THE ARAMAIC DIALECTS

Within the Semitic languages Aramaic belongs to the North West Semitic group which comprises Ugaritic, Phoenician, Hebrew, and Moabite, besides Aramaic. Within this group it happens to be Aramaic that has the closest relationship to Arabic (Arabic and the Northwest Semitic group being designated "Central Semitic"—as opposed to South and to East Semitic). By the end of the second millennium BC two distinctive sub-groups among the Northwest Semitic languages had emerged, Aramaic and Canaanite, the later consisting of Phoenician, Hebrew, and Moabite (some scholars would classify Ugaritic, too, as Canaanite). The following diagram indicates how the different Semitic languages are related to one another:

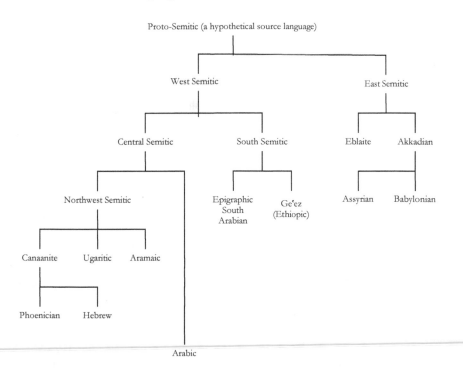

19

The term "Aramaic" in fact covers a multitude of different dialects, ranging in time from the early first millennium BC (isolated inscriptions) to the present day when various modern Aramaic dialects are still spoken in certain areas of Syria, Eastern Turkey, Iraq, Iran, and the Caucasus—and among several of the emigré communities. A considerable number of different written dialects of Aramaic are known from inscriptions, but only in three cases do extensive literatures survive. These were produced mainly in the course of the first millennium AD, by three different religious groups in the Middle East—Jews, Christians, and Mandeans; of these three, the Christian and Mandean dialects of Aramaic developed their own distinctive script, and it is largely for that reason that these two dialects have come to be called by the separate names of "Syriac" and "Mandaic." The various dialects of Jewish Aramaic, on the other hand, were written in the form of the old Aramaic script which was adopted by the Jews after the exile for writing Hebrew (and hence now known as "square Hebrew," as opposed to the older "palaeo-Hebrew" script). Today it is customary to use "square Hebrew" in printing all dialects of Aramaic other than Syriac and Mandaic (although texts from both these dialects have occasionally also been printed in Hebrew script).

The correct classification of the Aramaic dialects remains a matter of dispute among scholars, and the following division of the dialects into five chronological groups follows the general schema put forward by J. A. Fitzmyer:

(1) *Old Aramaic.* This comprises the oldest surviving texts in Aramaic; all are inscriptions, and among them are the famous Sefire treaty texts. This period, when several different dialects are already discernible, is generally regarded as lasting from the tenth to the end of the eighth century BC (it should be remembered, of course, that the dividing lines between the different periods are inevitably somewhat arbitrary).

(2) *Official Aramaic* (sometimes also known as Imperial Aramaic, or Reichsaramäisch). Under the late Assyrian and Neo-Babylonian empires Aramaic came to be used more and more as a chancery language. This is well illustrated by an Assyrian wall painting depicting two scribes taking down records: one scribe is writing cuneiform Akkadian with a stylus, while the other is writing Aramaic, using a pen. Aramaic thus came to be the official language of empire inherited by the Achaemenids. From this period (sixth to fourth century BC) we have both inscriptions on stone and, from Egypt, documents and letters on papyrus and leather deriving from three different archives, the most famous of which is the Jewish one from

Elephantine. Of the other two archives, one belongs to the Persian Satrap, while the other one consists of private correspondence. In recent years a further archive of official documents in Aramaic has turned up in Afghanistan, indicating how widely the language had spread. The Aramaic of the book of Ezra in its essentials belongs to this period.

(3) *Middle Aramaic.* The various texts that survive from the half millennium following Alexander's conquests in the Middle East (in other words, the Hellenistic and early Roman Empire, up to about AD 200) are today often lumped together as "Middle Aramaic"; in fact the dialects represented are very disparate, for, on the one hand there are archaizing literary texts like the Aramaic of Daniel and some of the fragmentary Qumran texts in Aramaic, while on the other hand, there are the various local dialects, known mainly from inscriptions, which emerged around the turn of the Christian era at various points on the edge of the fertile crescent—Petra (Nabatean), Palmyra (Palmyrene), Hatra, and Edessa (the earliest pagan Syriac inscriptions belong to this period). From further away, Armenia, Georgia, and Afghanistan, come other inscriptions in what is often a very corrupt form of Aramaic.

(4) *Late Aramaic.* The period spanning the later Roman Empire and the beginnings of Arab rule (approximately AD 200–700) saw the emergence of a distinct division between Eastern and Western dialects of Aramaic. Western Aramaic includes Samaritan Aramaic, various Palestinian Jewish Aramaic dialects, and Christian Palestinian Aramaic (also known as Palestinian Syriac, since it employs the Syriac Estrangelo script). Eastern Aramaic comprises Mandaic, Babylonian Jewish Aramaic dialects, and Syriac (what emerged as the classical literary dialect of Syriac differs in some small details from the Syriac of the earlier pagan inscriptions from the Edessa area).

(5) *Modern Aramaic.* The Arab conquests effected the gradual elimination of Aramaic as a spoken language in most areas, and it is only in outlying mountainous regions that Aramaic has survived up to the present day, spoken by small groups of Christians, Jews, Mandaeans and a few Muslims. A Western Aramaic dialect survives only in three villages in the Anti-Lebanon (two Muslim, and one—Ma'lula—Christian), although the accounts of seventeenth- and eighteenth-century travellers indicate that it was much more widespread a few centuries ago. Eastern Aramaic dialects, however, enjoy a rather wider use: a few Jewish dialects from northern Iraq and Iran are is still spoken by some immigrants to Israel from that region,

while several different Christian dialects are still in common use in the mountainous area formed today by eastern Turkey, northern Iraq, northwestern Iran, and Azerbaijan. In the area of southeastern Turkey known as Tur Abdin the local Syrian Orthodox Christians employ a dialect called Turoyo, the "mountain" language, which until recently was hardly ever written; now, however, its written form is being promoted in parts of the diaspora. In Iraq, Iran, and Azerbaijan the Chaldeans and East Syrians speak a rather different dialect (or rather, group of dialects); this is sometimes also written. It has already been mentioned that the earliest written texts in Modern Syriac, belonging to the seventeenth century, come from the Alqosh area in northern Iraq, while it was the dialect of Urmia that was subsequently promoted, in the nineteenth century, with the establishment there by the American Presbyterian mission of a printing press. That the dialect spoken in Iraq (variously called Fellihi, Soureth, or Swadaya) is still a force for politicians to take note of was shown by the action of the Iraqi government in 1972 when, in a decree of the 22 April, it granted "cultural rights to the Assyrian, Chaldean, and Syrian Orthodox citizens who speak Syriac." Unfortunately this decree was only put into effect in a very limited way.

In the last few decades two factors have led to a blossoming of publications in Modern Syriac: the large-scale emigration to western countries has meant that new possibilities for publishing in minority languages such as Modern Syriac have been opened up, and this has been made economically viable by the facilities for printing Syriac scripts using computer technology.

Classical Syriac emerges as an independent Aramaic dialect in the early first century AD, and is first attested in a pagan inscription dated AD 6, from Birecik on the river Euphrates, some 45 miles west of Edessa (whose modern name, Urfa, is derived from the Syriac Urhay), the cultural centre of Syriac literature. To early writers Syriac is actually known as "Edessene," an indication that it started out simply as the local Aramaic dialect of Edessa. That it came to be adopted as the literary language of Aramaic-speaking Christians all over Mesopotamia may in part be due to the prestige enjoyed by Edessa thanks to its claim to possess a letter written by Jesus to its king (of Arab stock) named Abgar the Black (this was already translated into Greek, around AD 300, by Eusebius in his *Ecclesiastical History*, I.13).

It is a remarkable fact that written Syriac, in the form that had become standardized by the fourth century, differs hardly at all in morphology from the written classical Syriac still employed today by Syrian Orthodox clergy and some others. Nevertheless, although the language remained the same, there emerged two different pronunciations of Syriac, usually known as the "Eastern" and the "Western." The Eastern, which is essentially the more archaic, came to be used by members of the Church of the East, living mainly in what is now Iraq and Iran, while the Western is employed in the Maronite and the Syrian Orthodox traditions whose homeland is further west (mainly modern Syria and southeastern Turkey). The most obvious difference between the two consists in the pronunciation of original *a*: the Eastern pronunciation preserves it (e.g., *malka*, "king"), while the Western alters it to *o* (*malko*).

SYRIAC SCRIPTS

The earliest Syriac inscriptions of the first and second centuries AD (all pagan) employ a script with many similarities to Palmyrene cursive writing, but by the time of our earliest manuscripts (early fifth century AD) this script has taken on a more formalized character, known as "Estrangelo" (probably from Greek *strongulos*, "rounded"). The British Library preserves many superb pieces of calligraphy in this hand. Although the script continued to be used well into the Middle Ages (and indeed enjoyed a dramatic local revival in Tur Abdin in the eleventh and twelfth centuries), during the course of the eighth century there emerged, side by side with it, a new and more compact script which had developed from an earlier cursive script, known from three legal documents from the early 240s and a few colophons, or end notes, by scribes of manuscripts otherwise written in Estrangelo. The new script is known as *serto* (literally "a scratch, character"), though in older European works it is often designated "Jacobite," since it became the normal script employed by the "Jacobites" (i.e., Syrian Orthodox); it is in fact also used by the Maronites as well. A few centuries later, among the East Syrians, we see the gradual emergence from Estrangelo of the other main Syriac script, today employed by Chaldeans and Assyrians. This East Syriac script has likewise in the past usually been called the "Nestorian" or "Chaldean" script by European writers. From about the eleventh century onwards a third distinctive script associated with a particular ecclesiastical community developed, the Melkite; this was employed by scribes of the Chalcedonian Patriarchate of Antioch.

The study of Syriac palaeography is still in its infancy, and the dating of manuscripts on the basis of the hand alone can be a matter of great uncertainty. The only guidance available is the excellent collection of photographs in W. H. P. Hatch's *An Album of Dated Syriac Manuscripts*

(Boston, 1946; now reissued with an important new introductory chapter by L. van Rompay, Piscataway NJ, 2002).

The early centuries of Arab rule witnessed the emergence of various vocalization systems to assist the reading and pronunciation of the unvowelled Arabic, Hebrew, and Syriac scripts. For Syriac we know that one of the early experimenters in this field was the great Syrian Orthodox scholar Jacob of Edessa, fragments of whose grammar, setting out his suggestions, survive. What finally emerged were two different systems, one used by Syrian Orthodox and Maronites (the so-called Jacobite vowel signs), and the other employed by East Syrians (the so-called Nestorian vowel signs); the former consist of symbols derived from Greek letters, the latter of different combinations of dots. In practice today West Syrian scribes (using Serto) rarely bother to insert the vowel signs, while East Syrian ones quite frequently give them.

Many Syriac scribes, right up to the present day (as we shall see, manuscripts still continue to be copied), have been very fine calligraphers. A few have also been illuminators, and by far the most famous illustrated Syriac manuscript is the so-called "Rabbula Gospels" in the Laurentian Library, Florence. According to the long colophon the scribe Rabbula completed this magnificent work on the sixth of February "in the year 897 of Alexander," that is AD 586, at the Monastery of St. John of Beth Zagba, somewhere in Syria. But this is by no means the only illuminated Syriac manuscript to survive, as can be readily seen by anyone who consults Jules Leroy's *Les manuscripts syriaques à peintures* (two volumes, one of text, one of plates; Paris, 1964).

V. TOOLS

In any academic discipline it essential to discover what are the main tools of the trade. Likewise it is important to learn how to find one's way around the secondary literature, and to distinguish which are likely to be the best reference books, and what are the most reliable sources of information on specific topics. Here some guidance is offered in a selection of important areas.[9]

A. GRAMMARS

These are best divided into two categories, elementary and reference grammars:

Elementary Grammars

There are now a number of helpful beginner's grammars in English, all provided with exercises and glossaries. J. F. Coakley's revision of *Robinson's Paradigms and Exercises in Syriac Grammar* (Oxford, 2002) has introduced many improvements into this long-lived and useful work. Other such works include J. F. Healey's *Leshono Suryoyo. First Studies in Syriac* (1980; revised edition with accompanying CD, Piscataway NJ, 2005), T. Muraoka's *Classical Syriac for Hebraists* (Wiesbaden, 1987), and W. M. Thackston's *An Introduction to Syriac* (Bethesda, 1999). While most elementary grammars use Serto script, that by Thackston employs Estrangelo, and the vocalization is provided by means of transcriptions. A recent very helpful introduction is provided by George Kiraz in his *The New Syriac Primer* (Second Edition, with downloadable material; Piscataway NJ, 2013). Another very handy reference tool is his *Verbal Paradigms in Syriac* (2010). Since different elementary grammars set out the material in differing ways, it can be helpful to make use of several different elementary grammars at the same time.

---

[9] Specifically aimed at Byzantinists, a summary guide to Syriac Studies is to be found in my "Syriac Sources and Resources for Byzantinists", in E.Jeffreys (ed.), *Proceedings of the 21st International Congress of Byzantine Studies, London 2006*, I, Plenary Papers (Aldershot, 2006), pp. 193–210.

Comparable beginner's grammars in other languages include: for German, A. Ungnad, *Syrische Grammatik* (2nd ed., Munich, 1932; repr. Hildesheim, 1992) is particularly well set out and has an interesting selection of texts (with a glossary); for French, there is Frey's *Petite grammaire syriaque* (Fribourg, 1984), which uses (vocalized) Estrangelo; and two recent grammars serve for Italian and Spanish readers: M. Pazzini, *Grammatica siriaca* (Jerusalem, 1999), and J. Ferrer i Costa and M. A. Nogueras, *Manual de gramática siríaca* (Barcelona, 1999). Even more recently a beginner's grammar in Armenian by A. Akopian (Erevan, 2003), and one in Polish (by A. Tronina and M. Szmajdzinski, 2003), have appeared, a gratifying indication of the ever widening appeal that Syriac studies are acquiring!

It is often helpful to start on reading simple vocalized texts at an early stage: for such purposes the grammatical analysis of the Peshitta Gospels in old tools like H. F. Whish's *Clavis Syriaca* (London, 1883) will be especially helpful to those learning the language on their own. Much shorter, but similarly conceived, and with a brief introductory grammatical sketch, are the *Syriac Reading Lessons*, by "The Author of The Analytical Hebrew and Chaldee Lexicon etc.," in other words B. Davidson (London, 1851).

Mention should also be made of some elementary books designed for teaching Syriac to schoolchildren (as opposed to older students). G. Kiraz's *The Syriac Primer* (Sheffield, 1988) has the benefit of an accompanying tape; his more recent *The Syriac Alphabet for Children* (Piscataway NJ, 2004) is aimed at teaching the basic shapes of the letters to young children. One from the Middle East that makes use of English as well as Arabic explanations is Asmar El-Khoury's *Companion* (Beirut, 1972).

Reference Grammars

Of intermediary sized grammars there are German ones by E. Nestle (with an English translation, Berlin, 1889) and by C. Brockelmann (Leipzig, 1899 and many subsequent editions); the latter in particular is very handy. Both these works also contain a selection of texts and a glossary. Of comparable size and coverage in French (but without any texts) is L. Costaz' *Grammaire syriaque* (Beirut, 2nd ed. 1964), where there is a useful typographical distinction between material meant for the less advanced and that reserved for the more experienced student.

The standard reference grammars are those by R. Duval, *Grammaire syriaque* (Paris, 1881) and (above all) T. Nöldeke, *Kurzgefasste syrische Grammatik* (Leipzig, 2nd ed. 1898); the German reprint of 1966 contains some supplements and an index of passages quoted, and these are included in the reissue of the English translation by J. A. Crichton, *Compendious Syriac*

Grammar (Winona Lake, 2001; the supplementary notes being translated by
P. T. Daniels), whose original edition was published in 1904. Although both
these works pay generous attention to syntax, there is actually a great need
for a specifically diachronic study of Syriac syntax. A much more recent
reference grammar is by T. Muraoka, *Classical Syriac. A Basic Grammar with a
Chrestomathy* (2nd ed., Wiesbaden, 2005); this also contains a select
bibliography on Syriac studies arranged under different topics. A great deal
of information, often difficult to discover elsewhere, can be found in
George Kiraz's *Turraṣ Mamlla. A Grammar of the Syriac Language.* Vol. 1,
Orthography (Piscataway NJ, 2012).

Of the older reference grammars, that by A. Merx, *Grammatica Syriaca*
(Halle, 1867), in Latin, might be singled out. An intriguing glimpse into the
earliest European grammars, produced during the Renaissance, is provided
by the facsimiles in W. Strothmann's *Die Anfänge der syrische Studien in Europa*
(Göttingen, 1971).[10]

It should not be forgotten that there are numerous grammars by native
Syriac scholars, going back to Jacob of Edessa in the seventh century. The
thirteenth-century polymath, Barhebraeus, even wrote a short verse
grammar, as well as a much more detailed one in prose. Of the more recent
grammars published in the Middle East mention should be made of the
Arabic one by C. J. David (Mosul, 1879; 2nd ed. 1896), the learned Syrian
Catholic metropolitan of Damascus and editor of the Mosul edition of the
Peshitta (1887–91), and of the French *Clef de la langue araméenne* (Mosul,
1905) by Alphonse Mingana, later of Birmingham fame.

It may come as a surprise that there are several modern grammars
produced in India. These are the work of scholars from the various Syriac
Churches in Kerala. The most extensive grammar is that by T. Arayathinal,
Aramaic Grammar (2 vols; Mannanam, 1957, 1959), running to over 1000
pages! This is in East Syriac script, and it includes extensive exercises (both
Syriac-English and English-Syriac; a key to them is provided at the end).
Ample illustrative examples are provided, and a particularly helpful feature
is the separate listing, in the table of contents, of the places in the course of
the grammar where questions of syntax are discussed. In the preface the
author (from the Syro-Malabar Church) tells how he had, throughout his
work, continually received encouragement, "though behind the curtain,"
from Mar Ivanios, the Archbishop of Trivandrum who had been the prime

---

[10] A summary overview of the history of Syriac scholarship in Europe will be
found in Section J, below.

mover in the creation (in 1930) of the Eastern Rite Catholic Syro-Malankara Church (which uses the West Syriac liturgical tradition).

Although Ariyathinal's grammar contains exercises, its length made it less suitable as a teaching grammar, and in Kerala this gap was filled by Gabriel of St. Joseph's *Syro-Chaldaic (Aramaic) Grammar* (7th ed., revised by Emmanuel [Thelly]; Mannanam, 1984). A useful feature of both these grammars is the provision of the Syriac grammatical terminology, alongside the English.

B. ANTHOLOGIES OF TEXTS (CHRESTOMATHIES)

The chrestomathy at the end of Brockelmann's *Syrische Grammatik* offers a particularly good selection of texts (there is a slight difference in choice of texts between the earlier and later editions), with samples in all three scripts, both vocalized and unvocalized. One of the pieces included is part of the *Teaching of Addai*, the Syriac account of the legend concerning king Abgar's correspondence with Jesus. Brockelmann's work contains a useful glossary, of which an English edition, with added etymological notes, has been published separately by M. Goshen Gottstein under the title *A Syriac Glossary* (Wiesbaden, 1970).

A new chrestomathy, with a wide variety of texts, together with brief introductions and with annotation is provided by M. Zammit, *ʿEnbe men Karmo Suryoyo (Bunches of Grapes from the Syriac Vineyard)—A Syriac Chrestomathy* (Piscataway NJ, 2006). Another recent selection of extracts is to be found in the Grammar by Akopian, mentioned above. Two other collections, from the middle of the last century, also deserve mention. R. Köbert's *Textus et Paradigmata Syriaca* (Rome, 1952) contains some twenty pages of paradigms followed by an interesting selection of texts, both biblical and non-biblical, in a handwritten Serto. A glossary to this is provided in his *Vocabularium Syriacum* (Rome, 1956), to which there is a supplement in *Orientalia* 39 (1970), pp. 315–19. A good variety of texts, in vocalized Serto script, is to be found in L. Costaz and P. Mouterde's *Anthologie syriaque* (Beirut, 1955). There are brief introductory notes on the authors represented.

Most of the older grammars contain chrestomathies at the end, and sometimes these will include texts not published elsewhere (e.g., the Syriac version of the *Lives of the Prophets* will be found in E. Nestle's grammar). There are also several nineteenth-century chrestomathies without grammars attached, and again many of these contain unpublished texts; of these the most important are by A. Rödiger (Halle/Leipzig, 3rd ed. 1892) and P. Zingerle (Rome, 1871–73).

From the Middle East there is a good graded series of reading books
(Serto) published in Qamishli (in eastern Syria; a modern town facing
ancient Nisibis, now Nuseybin across the border in Turkey): A. N.
Karabash, *Herge d-qeryana*, "Reading Exercises," in eight volumes (vol. 8,
1972). These contain several texts by contemporary Syriac authors.

Two older anthologies printed in the Middle East are of importance
since they include some texts not yet printed elsewhere. These are the
Kthabuna d-parthuthe, or "Little book of scraps," published by the
Archbishop of Canterbury 's mission at Urmia in 1898, and J. E. Manna's
Morceaux choisis de littérature araméenne (2 volumes; Mosul, 1901; reprinted
Baghdad, 1977). Both of these employ the East Syriac script.

C. DICTIONARIES

Besides the glossaries attached to the various grammars and chrestomathies
already mentioned, the beginner will also find W. Jenning's *A Lexicon to the
Syriac New Testament* (Oxford, 1926) particularly useful, seeing that one of
the most readily available vocalized Syriac texts is the British and Foreign
Bible Society's edition of the Peshitta New Testament (now reprinted by
the United Bible Societies). There are two further lexical aids for the
Peshitta New Testament: T. Falla's, *A Key to the Peshitta Gospels* I–II (Leiden,
1991, 2000), and G. Kiraz's *Lexical Tools to the Syriac New Testament* (JSOT
Manuals 7; Sheffield, 1994). The former, which has so far only reached the
letter *yodh*, is especially helpful for those with an interest in comparing the
Syriac with the Greek original. The prime feature of Kiraz's *Lexical Tools* lies
in the word frequency lists, ranging from the most frequent (1085–4234
times) down to those occurring just 10–11 times. Obviously students are
well advised to concentrate on the high flyers when learning vocabulary.
Other features are: a list of homographs occurring in the Peshitta New
Testament, convenient reference tables with paradigms of verbs, English
and Syriac indexes (each keyed to the word frequency list), and a skeleton
Syriac grammar, indicating the main structures, and providing a reverse
index of all the suffixes.

For those who read Italian, M. Pazzini's *Lessico concordanziale de Nuovo
Testamento Siriaco* (Jerusalem, 2004) will be found very helpful.

Of the dictionaries proper the three most easy to handle are Jessie
Payne Smith (Mrs. Margoliouth), *Compendious Syriac Dictionary* (Oxford, 1903
and many reprints), arranged alphabetically and very good for idioms; L.
Costaz, *Dictionnaire syriaque-français* (Beirut, 1963; repr. 1994), arranged by
root, and including English and Arabic equivalents as well as French; and
the *Gorgias Concise Syriac-English, English-Syriac Dictionary*, compiled by S.P.

Brock and G.A. Kiraz (Piscataway NJ, 2015), arranged alphabetically and based for the most part on the *Compendious Syriac Dictionary*. Any one of these should prove adequate for most practical purposes, but none of them gives any references to sources. If one is interested in attestation and sources, then one must consult the two monuments of Syriac lexicography, (Jessie's father) R. Payne Smith's *Thesaurus Syriacus*, and C. Brockelmann's *Lexicon Syriacum* (Berlin, 1895; much expanded second edition, 1928).

Brockelmann's *Lexicon* is a much more convenient size to handle, and it is in a single volume. Arrangement is by root and the language employed is Latin (at the end there is a useful reverse Latin-Syriac index; the second edition simply gives the page reference for the Syriac equivalent, but the first edition more conveniently provides the Syriac word itself). Lists of references, especially for rarer words, are very helpful, but quotations are never given, for reasons of space. A considerably adapted English translation and revision of Brockelmann's *Lexicon* by M. Sokoloff, the compiler of two invaluable dictionaries of Jewish Aramaic (Palestinian and Babylonian), is now available under the title *A Syriac Lexicon. A Translation from the Latin, Correction, Expansion, and Update of C. Brockelmann's Lexicon Syriacum* (Winona Lake/Piscataway NJ, 2009). This new edition has reordered the entries so that they are strictly alphabetical, and no longer arranged by root; it has also updated (and corrected) many of the references, above all where better editions are now available (especially important for Ephrem); the etymological notes are also considerably improved. Especially for English-speaking students of Syriac, this transformation of Brockelmann's *Lexicon* is an invaluable resource, in particular on those occasions when one needs to consult further that the three shorter dictionaries.

Robert Payne Smith's *Thesaurus Syriacus* in two folio volumes (Oxford, 1879, 1901) must be one of the most splendid of the many dictionaries which the Oxford University Press has put out: the beautiful headings and layout, with ample margins for annotation, are matched by the wealth of examples quoted. The work (which, like all dictionaries, draws on the fruits of many earlier dictionaries) employs Latin rather than English, and is arranged by root.

A *Supplement to the Thesaurus* of R. Payne Smith (Oxford, 1927) was compiled subsequently by his daughter Jessie, in order to include those texts which had been published for the first time only in the intervening years. Some further additions, mainly taken from medical texts, will be found in *Orientalia* 8 (1939), pp. 25–58.

Both Brockelmann and Payne Smith (father and daughter) made good use of the tenth-century Syriac lexicographers, Bar Bahlul (ed. R. Duval, 1888–91) and Bar 'Ali (Part 1 ed. G. Hoffmann, 1874; part II by R. J. H. Gottheil, 1908). The advanced student will find that these two works are sometimes worth consulting in their own right.

Of the older European dictionaries, E. Castell's *Lexicon Heptaglotton* (London, 1669 and reprints), based on Walton's Polyglot, and C. Schaaf, *Lexicon Syriacum Concordantiale* (Leiden, 2nd ed. 1717) still have their uses. Schaaf covers only the New Testament, but effectively acts as a concordance to this.

There are also several Syriac dictionaries published in the Middle East; of these the following deserve particular mention since they sometimes include words absent from the European dictionaries: G. Cardahi, *Al-Lobab, sive Dictionarium Syro-Arabicum* (2 volumes; Beirut, 1887–91); T. Audo, *Dictionnaire de la langue chaldéenne* (Syriac-Syriac, in 2 volumes; Mosul, 1897; several recent reprints); and J. E. Manna, *Vocabulaire chaldéen-arabe* (Mosul, 1900), reprinted, ed. R. J. Bidawid, as *Chaldean-Arabic Dictionary*, with a new appendix, pp. 856–986 (Beirut, 1975). Of these, Audo's *Dictionnaire* is particularly useful, and it served as the basis for the most recent large-scale dictionary, by the learned Indian Syriac scholar, E. Thelly, *Syriac-English-Malayalam Lexicon* (Kottayam, 1999). Very recently another impressive Syriac-Syriac dictionary has been published; this is the *Key of Language: Syriac Dictionary/Qlido d-leshono. Leksiqon Suryoyo*, by Yuyaqim d-Beth Yahqub (St Augin Monastery Press, 2016). The compiler is the refounder and abbot of the Monastery of St Augin in south-east Turkey, and his very detailed work is an astonishing achievement.

A large number of important Syriac texts have been published since almost all these dictionaries were compiled and, because these newly edited texts sometimes include words or formations not yet recorded in any of available dictionaries, there is certainly ample room for at least another supplement to the *Thesaurus*!

All the dictionaries mentioned so far confine themselves to pre-modern texts in Classical Syriac. Since Classical Syriac still functions actively as a literary language (variously known as *ktobonoyo* when spoken, and Modern Literary Syriac when written),[11] and since the modern world

---

[11] This is the term used by E. Wardini, "Neologisms in Modern Literary Syriac," *Mélanges de l'Université Saint Joseph* 53:5 (1993/4), pp. 401–566, 54 (1995/6), pp. 167–324. For the term *ktobonoyo*, see G.A. Kiraz, "Kthobonoyo Syriac: some observations and remarks", *Hugoye* 10:2 (2007), pp. 129–142. For the general

requires the creation of many new usages and numerous neologisms, there is a great need for new dictionaries to cover these. Several beginnings have been made by different enthusiasts for the language, though none yet are Syriac-English. Of those serving other languages the following are substantial (it is impressive that three come from Iraq):

- Şabo Hanna and Aziz Bulut, *Wörterbuch Deutsch-Aramäisch, Aramäisch-Deutsch* (Heilbronn, 2000), which runs to over 900 pages.

- Odisho M. Giwargis Ashita, *Hilqa deLeshana. Assyrian* [Syriac]-*Arabic Dictionary* (Baghdad, 1997); at the end (pp. 590–705) there is a useful Syriac-Arabic-English glossary of scientific, medical, and other technical terms).

- Younan Hozaya and Anderios Youkhana, *Bahra. Arabic-Assyrian Dictionary* (Erbil, 1998).

- Shlemon Esho Khoshaba and Emanuel Youkhana, *Zahreera. Arabic-Syriac Dictionary* (Duhuk, 2000).

- Gabriel Afram, *Svensk assyrisk ordbok* (Stockholm, 2005). This detailed Swedish-Syriac dictionary, compiled by a noted author writing in Modern Literary Syriac, runs to 1242 pages.

Besides the English-Syriac section of the *Gorgias Syriac-English, English-Syriac Dictionary*, there is another for English-Syriac which also covers modern usage: Zeki Zitun, *Bukhro. English to Syriac Dictionary* (Australia, 2007)

The different names given to Syriac in these dictionaries reflect the arguments in the different communities of Syriac tradition over how they should describe themselves in a modern secular world. Although useful, none of these dictionaries could be described as a scientific work of lexicography (and none, of course, give any references). One day, no doubt a long way off in the future, it would be a fascinating and very worthwhile task to compile a dictionary to cover this material, based on a representative collection of texts.

One of the main problems facing those writing in Classical Syriac today is posed by the need to provide terms for everyday items of the modern world. This is topic of an interesting work entitled *Tawldotho, or*

---

background, see my "Some observations on the use of Classical Syriac in the late twentieth century," *Journal of Semitic Studies* 34 (1989), pp. 363–75.

Syriac Neologisms. Principles—Criteria & Examples (Aleppo, 1997), by Abrohom Nouro (1923–2009), one of the main proponents of the use of Classical Syriac as both a written and a spoken language.[12]

A complete list of all Syriac dictionaries ever published has been compiled by D.G.K. Taylor, *An Annotated Bibliography of Printed Syriac Lexica* (Piscataway NJ, forthcoming). A short introduction to the topic can by found in my "Syriac Lexicography: reflections on resources and sources," *Aramaic Studies* 1 (2003), pp. 165–78 (also reprinted in A.D. Forbes and D.G.K. Taylor (eds.), *Foundations for Syriac Lexicography* (Piscataway NJ, 2005), pp. 195–208.).

D. THE BIBLE IN SYRIAC

New Testament

The beginner will find the British and Foreign Bible Society's edition of the *Peshitta New Testament* (1920) extremely useful for reading practice: it is very clearly printed and is fully vocalized (Serto with West Syriac vowel signs). The text has been reprinted many times, and two forms are currently widely available: the United Bible Societies' *Syriac New Testament and Psalms*, and in the New Testament section of their *Syriac Bible* (1988 and subsequent reprints; the first edition, of 1979, reprinted a different edition of the New Testament text, that by S. Lee).

This edition also has the advantage that it contains a reliable text, and for the Gospels it is based on the critical edition by Pusey and Gwynn (1901); the latter has a facing Latin translation and gives the variant readings (usually of a very minor character) from a number of early manuscripts). Since the original Syriac New Testament Canon did not contain 2 Peter, 2 and 3 John, Jude, or Revelation, there is no Peshitta translation of these books available; as a result the Bible Society prints a later translation, probably belonging to the sixth century, for these particular books.

A good way to familiarize oneself with reading unvocalized texts is to read the edition of the Peshitta New Testament in Estrangelo script, published by The Way International under the title *The Aramaic New Testament* (New Knoxville, 1983) alongside one of the vocalized editions. Once familiar with Estrangelo script, a very instructive thing to do is to study the three different versions of the Syriac Gospels, the Old Syriac, the Peshitta, and the Harklean, which are very conveniently juxtaposed in

---

[12] On this see E. E. Knudsen, "An important step in the revival of Literary Syriac: Abrohom Nuro's Tawldotho," *Oriens Christianus* 84 (2000), 59–65.

G. Kiraz's *Comparative Edition of the Syriac Gospels: Aligning the Sinaiticus, Curetonianus, Peshitta and Harklean Versions* (4 vols, Leiden, 1996). After reading only a few verses it will become obvious how fashions in biblical translation have radically changed between the time of the Old Syriac (probably early third century) and the Harklean (early seventh century).

Kiraz derived his texts from the best available editions. In the case of the two Old Syriac manuscripts these were F. C. Burkitt, *Evangelion da-Mepharreshe* (Cambridge, 1904), for the Curetonian manuscript (with variations of the Sinaiticus at the bottom of the page in the apparatus; the smaller sized Estrangelo type in the notes is actually based on Burkitt's own beautiful Syriac handwriting, itself based on the earliest dated Syriac literary manuscript, copied in Edessa in November 411); and A. S. Lewis, *The Old Syriac Gospels* (London, 1910) for the Sinaiticus (also giving the variations in the Curetonianus). Since the Sinaiticus (not to be confused with the famous Greek manuscript known by the same name!) is a palimpsest, with the Old Syriac as the largely erased undertext, it is likely that eventually much more of its text will become legible, once new techniques for reading palimpsests have been satisfactorily developed. A forthcoming Synopsis of the Syriac Gospels, by D.G.K. Taylor, will make use, not only of new multispectral images of the undertext of Sinaitus Syrus, but also of what remains of the third Old Syriac Gospel manuscript which has recently come to light in St Catherine's Monastery, Sinai.

While Pusey and Gwynn's edition was at hand for the Peshitta, Kiraz's text of the Harklean was specially provided by A. Juckel, using one of the oldest available manuscripts, written less than a century after the revision had been undertaken. This was because the text of the Harklean in the old edition by J. White was taken from a much later and less satisfactory manuscript. White's edition of the complete Harklean New Testament, published under the misleading title of *Versio Syriaca Philoxeniana* (2 vols, 1778, 1803) still remains the only edition for Acts (where the Harklean is an especially important witness), but for most other books it has now been replaced by the recent edition of the major Catholic Epistles and the Pauline Letters by B. Aland and A. Juckel (*Das Neue Testament in Syrische Überlieferung*, I, II.1–3; Berlin, 1986–2002). This splendid comparative edition provides not only the text of the Peshitta and the Harklean (based on the oldest manuscripts), but it also gives the text of quotations to be found in later Syriac writers.

An edition of the Peshitta New Testament, well provided with cross-references and other notes, has also been produced by the Monastery of St

Gabriel in Tur 'Abdin (south-east Turkey), entitled 'the Peshitta of Mardin' (2007).

A collection of Syriac quotations from, or probably from, the Diatessaron (Gospel harmony) was made by I. Ortiz de Urbina, *Vetus Evangelium Syrorum; Diatessaron Tatiani*, as volume VI of the Madrid Polyglot (1967); although this appeared after the first part of the Syriac manuscript with Ephrem's Commentary on the Diatessaron had been published by L. Leloir (1963), it now needs supplementing from the more recently published section of the manuscript (1990). Expert guidance on the many hazards and problems connected with the study of the Diatessaron is to be found in W. Petersen's *Tatian's Diatessaron* (Leiden, 1994).

There are several English translations of the Peshitta New Testament, or parts of it: by J. Murdock (1851), W. Norton (1890), and G. M. Lamsa (1933); none of these is satisfactory, and the only reliable English translations are that of the Old Syriac Gospels by F. C. Burkitt (in his edition of the Curetonian), and those published in the Gorgias Press's bilingual series, Syriac-English, the Antioch Bible.

For a long time Schaaf's New Testament lexicon (listed under *Dictionaries*, above) was the nearest thing to a concordance to the Syriac New Testament. Despite its title, *The Concordance to the Peshitta Version of the Aramaic New Testament*, published by The Way International (New Knoxville, 1985), this turns out to be a word list, giving references to the different main grammatical forms; though useful as such, it does not have the wonderful convenience of a concordance proper. Several beginnings had been made in the past on compiling such a concordance, but it was only when someone who combined expertise in both Syriac and computing took up the task that a real concordance to the Syriac New Testament finally appeared: this was G. Kiraz's magnificent *A Computer-Generated Concordance to the Syriac New Testament* (Leiden, 1993), in six volumes (the last two consist of various useful appendices). The Syriac colophon at the end of the final volume will reveal (among other things) who won the Oxford versus Cambridge Boat Race on the River Thames in 1992. A more compact form of this invaluable work is in preparation. The Old Syriac Gospels are now served by *A Key-Word-in-Context Concordance*, produced by J. Lund, in collaboration with G. Kiraz (3 vols, Piscataway NJ, 2004).

Old Testament: Peshitta

For the Peshitta Old Testament there is the convenient United Bible Societies' edition of the whole Syriac Bible. This is in fact a reprint of the edition by S. Lee, published in 1823. Early in the twentieth century good editions of the Pentateuch (Estrangelo) and Psalms (Serto, unvocalized) were published, and the latter (now vocalized) appears in the United Bible Societies' edition of the *Syriac New Testament and Psalms*.

Currently a large-scale new edition of the Peshitta Old Testament, based on early manuscripts, is in the course of publication by the Peshitta Institute (Leiden/Amsterdam); so far the following volumes have appeared:

Sample edition: Song of Songs, Tobit, IV Ezra (1966)
I.1: Genesis, Exodus (1977)
I.2 & II.1b: Leviticus, Numbers, Deuteronomy, and Joshua (1991)
II.1a: Job (1982)
II.2: Judges, Samuel (1978)
II.3: Psalms (1980)
II.4: Kings (1976)
II.5: Proverbs, Wisdom, Qohelet (Eccl.), Song of Songs (1979)
III.1: Isaiah (1987)
III.3: Ezekiel (1985)
III.4: XII Prophets, Daniel (1980)
IV.2: Chronicles (1998)
IV.3: Apocalypse of Baruch, IV Ezra (1973)
IV.4: Ezra, Nehemiah; I-II Maccabees (2014)
IV.6: Odes, Psalms of Solomon, Apocryphal Psalms, Tobit, I (III) Ezra (1972).

These are beautifully printed in Estrangelo script; the edition makes use of all known early manuscripts as well as of many later ones. As its basic text, the earliest complete Peshitta Old Testament manuscript, in the Ambrosian Library, Milan, is employed; as its designation (7a1) indicates, it dates from the seventh century (the first number gives the century, the letter indicates the category—here, complete Old Testament—and the third the serial number within the category). Since all the editions of the Peshitta Old Testament published from seventeenth to the nineteenth century were based on late manuscripts, it is essential to use the Leiden edition if one is interested in the relationship of the Peshitta to the Hebrew original; since the current United Bible Societies' edition reprints Lee's nineteenth-century edition, this caveat also applies there as well).

There are also reliable editions of several individual books: Psalms (W. Barnes, 1904); Lamentations (B. Albrektson, 1963); Wisdom of Solomon (J. A. Emerton, 1959); Ben Sira (Ecclesiasticus; N. Calduch-Benages, J. Ferrer, and J. Liesen, 2003, with English and Spanish translations), and the Apocrypha (P. de Lagarde, 1861).

Of the old editions containing the entire Peshitta Old Testament, that of S. Lee (London, 1823), using Serto script, can sometimes be picked up second-hand; it is largely based on Brian Walton's London Polyglot Bible (1657), which in turn goes back to the Paris Polyglot of 1645. The manuscripts employed for these editions were mostly of very late West Syrian provenance, though Lee made some use of the twelfth century "Buchanan Bible," which had been brought back from India by the Reverend Claude Buchanan and presented to the University Library, Cambridge, around 1809.

The American Presbyterian Mission printed an edition at Urmia (north-west Iran) in 1852 containing the entire Peshitta Old Testament; for this, local East Syrian manuscripts were used as the basis, and the script employed is also East Syrian. A revision of this, made by Joseph de Kelayta, was published by the Trinitarian Bible Society in 1913 (printed in rather diminutive East Syrian characters; this has been reprinted a number of times).

A second Middle Eastern edition, prepared by the Syrian Catholic bishop C. J. David, was published by the Dominican press at Mosul, 1887–92; for this East Syrian script (vocalized) was employed. This edition was reprinted at Beirut in 1951. A handsome facsimile reprint, in three volumes, of the original edition has been published by the Gorgias Press (Piscataway NT, 2010). If one is looking for a vocalized text of the Bible in East Syriac script, this edition will serve the purpose well.

Mention should also be made of the magnificent photolithographic reproduction of the seventh-century manuscript of the Peshitta in the possession of the Ambrosian Library in Milan (7a1); for this, A. M. Ceriani was responsible (1876–79). A facsimile edition of this is now available from the Gorgias Press (2013, with an Introduction by E. Vergani).

Since there is generally very little variation between Peshitta manuscripts (at least compared with Septuagint ones), for most purposes it will make little difference which edition of the Peshitta Old Testament is used, although, as mentioned above, for any serious work on the Hebrew text underlying the Peshitta use of the Leiden edition is absolutely essential, since the text of the Peshitta evidently underwent some small but important modifications during the course of its history.

Two English translations of the Peshitta Old Testament are in the course of appearing, book by book. That sponsored by the Peshitta Insitute, and based on the Institute's critical editions, is aimed more at an academic public, while the Gorgias Press's bilingual Antioch Bible is meant for a wider readership: its text is specifically based on the Mosul Bible of

1887–1892, but the script has been altered to the West Syriac, with full vocalization. An impressive number of individual volumes of the Antioch Bible, covering books of both the Old and New Testament, have already appeared.

Old Testament: Syrohexapla and Other Syriac Versions

For the Syrohexapla A. M. Ceriani produced a photolithographic edition (1874) of a ninth-century manuscript in the Ambrosian Library containing the second half of the Old Testament (Job–Malachi). The companion volume to this manuscript was still in existence in the sixteenth century and was used by various Renaissance scholars; subsequently, however, it disappeared in circumstances still unknown. Other scattered Syrohexapla texts containing books from the first half of the Old Testament were collected together and edited by P. de Lagarde (*Bibliothecae Syriacae*, [Göttingen, 1892]; an earlier edition of this [1880] employed Hebrew type). Some subsequent finds were published by W. Baars in *New Syrohexaplaric Texts* (Leiden, 1968, with a valuable introduction), while a photographic edition of a Pentateuch manuscript from southeastern Turkey has been published by A. Vööbus (Louvain, 1975). There is also a critical edition of *The Syrohexapla Psalter* (for which several manuscripts survive), by R. J. Hiebert (Atlanta, 1989).

Fragments of a sixth-century translation, made from the Septuagint, of certain books have been published by A. Ceriani, in *Monumenta Sacra et Profana*, vol. 5 (1875). A late seventh-century revision of certain books of the Peshitta, but making use of Greek manuscripts, was undertaken by Jacob of Edessa; this interesting combination of two traditions, Hebrew and Greek, of the same sacred text, can be studied in the recent edition (with English translation), *The Books of Samuel in the Syriac Version of Jacob of Edessa*, by A. G. Salvesen (Leiden, 1999).

Old Testament: Tools

There are concordances to the following parts of the Peshitta Old Testament:

Pentateuch: W. Strothmann, *Konkordanz zum syrischen Bibel. Der Pentateuch* (4 vols, Wiesbaden, 1986); and P. Borbone, J. Cook, K. Jenner, and D. M. Walter, *The Old Testament in Syriac, V. 1 Concordance. The Pentateuch* (Leiden, 1997). These two works complement one another; the latter is based on the Leiden edition, and indicates the corresponding Hebrew equivalents.

Historical and Wisdom books, with Ruth and Esther: W. Strothmann, *Konkordanz zum syrischen Bibel. Die Mautbe* (6 vols, Wiesbaden, 1995). The title refers to the name of a particular grouping of Old Testament books found in some manuscripts.

Psalms: N. Sprenger, *Konkordanz zum syrischen Psalter* (Wiesbaden, 1976).

Prophetical books: W. Strothmann, *Konkordanz zum syrischen Bibel. Die Propheten* (4 vols, Wiesbaden, 1984).

Hosea: P. G. Borbone and F. Mandracci, *Concordanze del testo siriaco di Osea* (Turin, 1987).

Ecclesiastes: W. Strothmann, *Konkordanz des syrischen Koheletbuches nach der Peshitta und der Syrohexapla* (Wiesbaden, 1973).

Ecclesiasticus: M. M. Winter, *A Concordance to the Peshitta Version of Ben Sira* (Leiden, 1976).

There is also a word list for the Apocrypha/Deuterocanonical books: W. Strothmann, *Wörterverzeichnis der apokryphen-deuterokanonischen Schriften des Alten Testaments in der Peshitta* (Wiesbaden, 1988).

An invaluable *List of Old Testament Peshitta Manuscripts* was published by the Peshitta Institute (Leiden) in 1961. A new edition is in preparation.

Bibliographies and Introductions

Bibliographies

The Peshitta Old Testament is well served by P. B. Dirksen, *An Annotated Bibliography of the Peshitta of the Old Testament* (Monographs of the Peshitta Institute, 5; Leiden, 1989), with a supplement (also by P. B. Dirksen) in P. B. Dirksen and A. van der Kooij (eds.), *The Peshitta as Translation. Papers read and the II Peshitta Symposium* (Monographs of the Peshitta Institute, 8; Leiden, 1995), pp. 221–36. Subsequent publications, for 1996–2010, can be most readily found in my *Syriac Studies. A Classified Bibliography*, vol 2. 1991–2010 (Patrimoine syriaque 7; Kaslik, 2014), pp. 77–112.

No comparable bibliography for the Peshitta New Testament (or for any of the other Syriac versions) exists, though fairly complete coverage can be gained by consulting the general bibliographies of Syriac studies listed below (Chapter V, G).

Introductions

There are a number of general introductions to the Bible in Syriac:

S. P. Brock, *The Bible in the Syriac Tradition* (2nd edn, Piscataway NJ, 2006). Among the translations of this book is one into Classical Syriac

(Piscataway NJ, 2002), by Augen Aydin (now Mor Polycarpus Aydin, Syrian Orthodox metropolitan of the Netherlands).

"The Bible in Syriac," in *The Hidden Pearl*, III (Rome, 2001), pp. 221–53.

M. van Esbroeck, "Les versions orientales de la Bible," in J. Kraşovec (ed.), *Interpretation of the Bible* (Ljubljana/Sheffield, 1998), pp. 399–509 (for Syriac: pp. 480–502).

Peshitta Old Testament:

P. B. Dirksen, "The Old Testament Peshitta," in M. J. Mulder (ed.), *Miqra. Text, Translation, Reading and Interpretation of the Hebrew Bible in Ancient Judaism and Early Christianity* (Assen, 1988), pp. 255–97.

La Peshitta del Antico Testamento (Brescia, 1993).

M. Weitzman, *The Syriac Version of the Old Testament. An Introduction* (Cambridge, 1999). This masterly work is much more than an ordinary introduction.

References to the considerable number of recent monographs on different books and aspects of the Peshitta Old Testament, often in the series Monographs of the Peshitta Institute Leiden, can readily be located in the bibliographies mentioned above.

Syriac New Testament:

The best introduction remains B. M. Metzger's *The Early Versions of the New Testament* (Oxford, 1977), where the first chapter is devoted to the Syriac versions. It should, however, be noted that the Philoxenian/Harklean problem, which he discusses, is now resolved: the surviving manuscripts represent the Harklean version, whereas the Philoxenian is lost, apart from quotations.

Biblical exegesis:

Two contributions by L. van Rompay to M. Saebø, *Hebrew Bible/Old Testament. History of its Interpretation*, I.i (Göttingen, 1996), pp. 612–41, and I.ii (2000), pp. 559–77, offer an excellent overview of the subject, and give good guidance for further reading. For the New Testament there is a helpful listing of the relevant Syriac authors and texts by J.C. McCullough, "Early Syriac Commentaries on the New Testament", *Near Eastern School of Theology: Theological Review* (Beirut) 5 (1982), 14–33, 79–126.

The Bible in Christian Palestinian Aramaic

By way of appendix to this section a word should be said about the Christian Palestinian Aramaic (or Palestinian Syriac) version of the Bible, made from Greek (in fact all the surviving texts in this dialect are translations from Greek). As has already been seen, this is a Western Aramaic dialect quite separate from Syriac, even though it uses an Estrangelo script. Only fragments of the version survive, often as the underwriting of palimpsest manuscripts. All the older manuscripts containing fragments of biblical books have recently been re-edited by C. Müller-Kessler and M. Sokoloff in their *A Corpus of Christian Palestinian Aramaic*, of which the following volumes have appeared so far:

> I, *The Christian Palestinian Aramaic Old Testament and Apocrypha Version from the Early Period* (Groningen, 1997),
>
> IIA and B, *Gospels; Acts of the Apostles and Epistles* (1998).
>
> III, *The Forty Martyrs of the Sinai Desert, Eulogius the Stone-Cutter, and Anastasia* (1996)
>
> V, *The Catechism of Cyril of Jerusalem* (1999).

For the New Testament the most extensive texts are in later Gospel Lectionaries (of the eleventh and twelfth century), and these were edited by the Scottish twin sisters A. S. Lewis and M. D. Gibson, *The Palestinian Syriac Lectionary of the Gospels* (London, 1899). C. Müller-Kessler has also written the standard grammar, *Grammatik des Christlich-Palästinisch-Aramäischen*, I (Hildesheim, 1991), while M. Sokoloff's *A Dictionary of Christian Palestinian Aramaic* (Leuven, 2014) replaces the earlier one by F. Schultess, *Lexicon Syropalaestinum* (Berlin, 1903).

E. HISTORIES OF SYRIAC LITERATURE

A number of recent introductions to Syriac literature are now available. Thanks to the initiative of a Maronite priest, Fr. Maroun Atallah, the Centre d'études et de recherches orientales (CERO) in Antelias (Lebanon) has recently published a very useful collective volume entitled *Nos sources. Arts et littératures syriaques* (Antelias, 2005), with contributions by an international group of scholars, written in English, French, and German. Since this provides chapters on all the most important genres and topics, it serves as a very helpful introduction to Syriac literature as a whole.

In English there is S. P. Brock, *A Brief Outline of Syriac Literature* (2nd edn, Piscataway, 2011), written originally for the M.A. Course in Syriac Studies at the St. Ephrem Ecumenical Research Institute in Kottayam, Kerala (affiliated to the Mahatma Ghandi University of Kottayam). This gives summary introductions to 100 Syriac authors (in chronological order) and to the main genres; some basic guidance on secondary literature in English is provided. Over half the book is devoted to short sample passages in translation from the more important writings. Guidance on the main editions can be found in the bibliography to T. Muraoka's, *Classical Syriac* (2nd ed., 2005), pp. 144–53.

A much more detailed and extensive introduction, but confined to Syrian Orthodox authors is Aphrem Barsoum's *The Scattered Pearls. A History of Syriac Literature and Sciences*, translated by M. Moosa (2nd revised edition, Piscataway NJ, 2003); there is also a German translation (Wiesbaden, 2012). Patriarch Ignatius Afrem Barsoum, who died in 1957, had an unrivalled knowledge of Syriac literature and he mentions many authors and works which do not feature in any of the western histories of Syriac literature. Although his references to manuscripts are not always as precise as one might have wished, his book serves as an essential supplement to the standard history of Syriac literature by A. Baumstark (for which, see below).

The French collaborative volume entitled *Christianismes orientaux. Introduction à l'étude des langues et des littératures* (Paris, 1993) has an excellent chapter on Syriac by M. Albert (pp. 299–372). Likewise excellent are two contributions in Italian by P. Bettiolo: "Lineamenti di Patrologia siriaca," in A. Quacquarelli (ed.), *Complementi interdisciplinari di Patrologia* (Rome, 1989), pp. 503–603; and "Letteratura siriaca," in A. di Berardino (ed.), *Patrologia* V, *Dal Concilio di Calcedonia (451) a Giovanni Damasceno. I Padri Orientali* (Genoa, 2000), 413–93. All three provide good bibliographical guidance.

In German, a recent volume in the Kohlhammer Taschenbücher (no. 587; 2004), entitled *Syrische Kirchenväter* and edited by W. Klein, and meant for the more general reader, has chapters on 18 important authors (or in one case, figure) in the three main ecclesiastical traditions (Chalcedonian, Church of the East, Syrian Orthodox).

None of these works, however, goes anywhere near replacing A. Baumstark's *Geschichte der syrische Literatur* (Bonn, 1922; repr. Berlin, 1968), which remains the standard reference work, indispensable for every serious student of Syriac literature. Unfortunately Baumstark's German style is notoriously difficult and the layout is not exactly reader-friendly, so that this is not the sort of book one would want to read from cover to cover. What renders it indispensable, however, is the provision, in the notes, of all the manuscripts for each work mentioned. Now, nearly a century later, these listings are in much need of considerable supplementation, in view of more recent catalogues of major collections of Syriac manuscripts, such as those in Birmingham (UK), Paris, St Catherine's Monastery (Sinai), Deir al-

Surian (Egypt), and those made available through the work of the Hill Museum and Manuscript Library (HMML), for which see below.

Of the older works on Syriac literature, perhaps still the best, and certainly the most readable, is R. Duval's *La littérature syriaque* (Paris, 3ʳᵈ ed. 1907), which treats the subject by genre; this now also available in English translation by O. Holmey, *Syriac Literature* (Piscataway NJ, 2013). W. Wright's *A Short History of Syriac Literature* (London, 1894; repr. Piscataway NJ, 2001) is now outdated as an introduction, but it remains useful for the more advanced student, since Wright had an exceptionally good knowledge of the texts, having previously catalogued the very large collection of Syriac manuscripts in the British Museum (now in the British Library); what Wright lacked, however, was any real appreciation of Syriac literature in its own right. Better known for his popular (but now outdated) *How Greek Science passed to the Arabs* (London, 1954), de Lacy O'Leary had earlier written a short, but rather dry, work entitled *The Syriac Fathers* (London, 1909).

Two further works from the first half of the twentieth century should be mentioned: prior to writing his great work of 1922, Baumstark contributed a good section on Syriac literature in his *Die christliche Literaturen des Osten* I (Leipzig, 1911). J. B. Chabot's *Littérature syriaque* (Paris, 1934) is a well-informed introduction, as one would expect from an experienced editor of Syriac texts.

For the dwindling number of Syriacists who read Latin, I. Ortiz de Urbina's *Patrologia Syriaca* (Rome, 2ⁿᵈ ed. 1965) is a very handy tool for reference, being a catalogue of the main theological writers and their works; its bibliographies, attached to each section, will be found very useful, though of course these now frequently need updating. A brief and necessarily selective survey of Syriac literature was contributed by A. Baumstark and A. Rücker to the *Handbuch der Orientalistik, III: Semitistik* (Leiden, 1954), pp. 169–204.

A very much older, reference work which is still of great value to the specialist is J. S. Assemani's *Bibliotheca Orientalis*, in three large volumes (Rome, 1719–28; repr. Piscataway NJ, 2002), where a volume each is devoted to "Orthodox," "Monophysite," and "Nestorian" writers. Generous excerpts from manuscripts in the Vatican library are given throughout; in several cases these excerpts still remain the sole published source available. At the beginning of volume III Assemani printed the important medieval catalogue of Syriac authors and their writings, compiled by ʿAbdishoʿ, the East Syriac metropolitan of Nisibis who died in 1318.

Most Western histories of Syriac literature give the impression that Syriac literature died out after the Mongol invasions. Only Baumstark gives a few subsequent writers. This impression is actually a totally false one, for classical Syriac has continued to be an important literary language right up to the present day. The extent of this more recent literature was almost totally unknown to European scholars until the publication of R. Macuch's *Geschichte der spät-und neusyrischen Literatur* (Berlin, 1976), which covers both literature in classical Syriac and that in Modern Syriac (first written down in the seventeenth century). (For some addenda and corrections see the review in the *Journal of Semitic Studies* 23 (1978), pp. 129–38).

Macuch in fact based his work very closely on three important histories of Syriac literature published in the Middle East. The first of these has already been mentioned, Afrem Barsaum's *Scattered Pearls*, originally published in Arabic in 1943, with an enlarged second edition in 1956. Macuch in fact used the Syriac translation, made by the late metropolitan of Mardin (southeastern Turkey), Mar Iuhannon Philoxenos Dolabani, himself a considerable Syriac scholar; this was published at Qamishli (Syria) in 1967. The second of the three works used by Macuch was Albert Abuna's *Adab al-lugha al-aramiyya*, "Aramean literature" (Beirut, 1970), also in Arabic, which is a fine general history of Syriac literature; while the third was P. Sarmas's *Tash'ita d-siprayuta atoreta*, "History of Assyrian [i.e., Syriac] literature" (Tehran, 1969–70), which is in modern Syriac and covers East Syriac writers. Dr. Sarmas, who died in 1972, was one of the foremost authorities on Syriac in Iran.

For those interested in seeing what Syriac scholars, both Western and Middle Eastern actually look like, the collection of photographs in Abrohom Nouro's *My Tour in the Parishes of the Syrian Church in Syria and Lebanon* (Beirut, 1967) is to be recommended. The author, whose family comes from Edessa, was a real enthusiast for the Syriac language and one whose energy and dynamism knew no bounds; both he and his wife, Antoinette, spoke Classical Syriac at home.[13]

---

[13] I first had the pleasure of first meeting Malfono (= Teacher) Abrohom Nuro in the mid-nineteen-sixties: it was early one morning at the Syrian Catholic Patriarchate in Charfet (Lebanon) where I was staying the night: having heard rumours that a European *mestaryono* ("syriacisant") was at large, he had taken a taxi out from Beirut at once and turned up only shortly after dawn. The poem which he wrote in honour of Arthur Vööbus can be found at the beginning of the Festschrift in his honour (for this, see Chapter V H).

F. THE HISTORICAL BACKGROUND

Since Syriac literature spans a wide area both in time and in space there is no single work that covers the historical background. For the home of Syriac, Edessa, an eminently readable work is J. B. Segal's *Edessa, the Blessed City* (Oxford, 1971; repr. Piscataway NJ, 2001); the author was an authority on the early pagan inscriptions and mosaics from the area, and he has explored some fascinating byways of local literary history in the course of writing this book.

The earliest history of Syriac Christianity is extremely obscure, thanks to the absence of good historical sources prior to the fourth century. The evaluation of the *Teaching of Addai*, which purports to describe the conversion of Edessa in the reign of King Abgar V, as a result of his correspondence with Jesus, has greatly differed among modern scholars: some reject it outright as containing nothing of historical value, while others see it as containing genuine elements, but which have been retrojected from the late second century to the time of the crucifixion. The former view was notably that of W. Bauer in the first chapter of his *Orthodoxy and Heresy in Earliest Christianity* (which originally came out in German in 1934, but whose second edition, of 1963, was eventually published in English translation, Philadelphia, 1971); in more recent years it has been developed by H. J. W. Drijvers. The second view is associated especially with the name of F. C. Burkitt, who has been followed by a number of (mainly English) scholars. A related issue is whether earliest Syriac Christianity derived from the hellenized Gentile Christian milieu of Antioch (as might be suggested by the earliest known Christian Syriac author, Bardaisan), or whether it was mediated more directly from a Jewish Christian community in Palestine. The evidence is conflicting, and perhaps one should see this not as a case of either the one, or the other explanation as being correct, but suppose that these two different strands existed side by side, the former affecting the ruling classes in Edessa, and the latter the wider population of the region. A discussion of the evidence can be found in my "Eusebius and Syriac Christianity" (1992), reprinted as Chapter II of *From Ephrem to Romanos* (Aldershot, 1999).

Once the fourth, and especially the fifth and sixth centuries, are reached, the picture becomes much clearer, and some coverage at least of Syriac Christianity within the Roman Empire is to be found in the standard histories of the Early Church and of Late Antiquity, of which there are now many. A historian of Late Antiquity who has paid considerable attention to Syriac soucres is F.G.B. Millar in his *A Greek Roman Empire. Power and Belief under Theodosius II (408–450)* (Berkeley, 2006), and more of relevance can be found among his collected articles, *Religion and Community in the Roman Near East: Constantine to Muhammad* (London, 2013), and *Empire, Church and Society in the Later Roman Near East* (Leuven, 2016). For the seventh century background, P. Booth's *Crisis of Empire: Doctrine and Dissent at the End of Late Antiquity* (Berkeley, 2014) is very helpful. One of the few works which deals specifically with the history of Syriac Christianity in this period is W. S. McCullough, *A Short History of Syriac Christianity to the Rise of Islam* (Chico, 1982).

There is a long tradition of Chronicles written in Syriac, written between the fifth and thirteenth centuries (inclusive); a general presentation of these can be found in E.-I. Yousif's *Les chroniqueurs syriaques* (Paris, 2002); in much more detail M. Debié's *L'écriture de l'hitoire en syriaque* (Louvain, 2015) is the essential guide. In English, a schematic survey can be found in Chapter 1 of my *Studies in Syriac Christianity* (Aldershot, 1992). A number of the Syriac Chronicles are now available in English translation, several in the Liverpool series Translated Texts for Historians:

> A.N. Palmer, *The Seventh Century in the West-Syrian Chronicles* (Liverpool, 1993). This includes a historical introduction by R. Hoyland, and a translation, by S.P. Brock, of the apocalyptic section of the Apocalypse of Pseudo-Methodius.

> W. Witakowski, *Pseudo-Dionysius of Tel-Mahre, Chronicle, Part III* (Liverpool, 1996). This late eighth-century Chronicle is now less cumbrously known as the Zuqnin Chronicle; Part III, covering the sixth century, is based on a lost part of John of Ephesus' *Church History*.

> A. Harrak, *The Chronicle of Zuqnin. Parts III and IV, AD 488–775* (Toronto, 1999). Part IV is especially important for the early Abbasid period.

> F.R. Trombley and J.W. Watt, *The Chronicle of Pseudo-Joshua the Stylite* (Liverpool, 2006). A local Edessene work incorporated into the late eighth-century Zuqnin Chronicle; it covers the years 494 to 506.

> A.H. Becker, *Sources for the Study of the School of Nisibis* (Liverpool, 2008). This includes all the main sources, apart from the Statutes,

for the famous East Syriac School of Nisibis which flourished especially in the sixth century.

G. Greatrex, C. Horn, R. Phenix, *The Chronicle of Pseudo-Zechariah Rhetor* (Liverpool, 2011). This sixth-century chronicle covers from the mid-fifth to the mid-sixth century.

M. Moosa, *The Syriac Chronicle of Michael Rabo (the Great)* (Teaneck NJ, 2014). The author of this extensive chronicle, starting from creation, was the Syrian Orthodox Patriarch who died in 1199. The Chronicle is of particular interest for the Crusader period.

D. Wilmshurst, *Bar Hebraeus, the Ecclesiastical Chronicle* (Piscataway NJ, 2016). He covers the history of the Chruch of the East up to the end of the fifth century, as well as that of the Syrian Orthodox Church.

A. Harrak, *The Chronicle of Zuqnin, Parts I and II. From Creation to the Year 506/7 AD* (Piscataway NJ, 2017)

For those interested in Syriac sources for the early Arab period, R. Hoyland's *Seeing Islam as others saw it: a Survey and Evaluation of Christian, Jewish and Zoroastrian Writings on Early Islam* (Princeton, 1997) is an excellent guide.

The East Syriac Tradition

Two excellent books cover the entire span of the history of the Church of the East: C. Baumer's *The Church of the East. An illustrated History of Assyrian Christianity* (London, 2006), and D. Wilmshurst, *The Martyred Church. A History of the Church of the East* (London, 2011). On a much briefer scale there is W. Baum and D. Winkler's *The Apostolic Church of the East. A Concise History* (London, 2003).

For the early history of the Church of the East as it existed under the Sasanid empire (roughly modern Iraq and Iran) there are two older English works: W. A. Wigram, *An Introduction to the History of the Assyrian Church, 100–640 AD* (London, 1910), and W. G. Young, *Patriarch, Shah and Caliph* (Rawalpindi, 1974). Wigram was a member of the Archbishop of Canterbury's mission to the Church of the East and he did a great deal to bring knowledge of that Church's plight to the English-reading public. For the period, of the origins of Christianity in Mesopotamia (where legends abound) neither of these two works is sufficiently critical, and a more reliable account will be found in J. M. Fiey's *Jalons pour une histoire de l'église en Iraq* (Louvain, 1970), which covers up to the seventh century. A more detailed history spanning the Persian period is J. Labourt's *Le christianisme dans l'empire perse* (Paris, 1904), a solid work which still retains its value. For the very earliest period two recent works by C. and F. Jullien (two twin sisters) are of particular relevance: *Apôtres des confins. Processus missionnaires chrétiens dans l'empire iranien* (Paris, 2002), and *Aux origines de l'église de Perse: les Actes de Mari* (Louvain, 2003).

The large body of Martyr Acts from the Sasanian period are gradually becoming more accessible thanks to translations. An important re-assessment of their significance, especially of those under Shapur II in the mid fourth century, is provided in R. Payne's *A State of Mixture: Christians, Zoroastrians, and Iranian Political Culture in Late Antiquity* (Berkeley, 2015).

For the Church of the East's history under the Abbasid caliphs, besides Young's book, there is an valuable work in French by J. M. Fiey, *Chrétiens syriaques sous les Abbasides, surtout à Bagdad (749–1258)* (Louvain, 1980); this focuses on the Patriarchs of the Church of the East. The most famous of these was Timothy I, whose extensive correspondence includes an account of a dialogue he had with the caliph al-Mahdi, the subject of H. Putman's, *L'Eglise et l'Islam sous Timothée I (780–823)* (Beirut, 1975). Timothy is also the subject of a fine study by V. Berti, *Vita e studi di Timoteo I patriarca Cristiano di Baghdad* (Paris, 2009).

As was mentioned earlier, ninth-century Baghdad was the scene of great intellectual ferment, with the translation into Arabic of Greek philosophical, medical and scientific texts. This involved close cooperation between Christian, Jewish and Muslim scholars, and it was especially in the earlier period of the "translation movement," promoted by the Abbasid Caliphs, that Syriac scholars played an essential role, translating first from Greek into Syriac, and thence into Arabic. Two recent French books provide an entry into this subject from a Syriac perspective: E. I. Yousif, *Les philosophes et traducteurs syriaques. D'Athènes à Bagdad* (Paris, 1997), and R. Le Coz, *Les médecins nestoriens au Moyen Âge: les maitres des arabes* (Paris, 2004).[14]

This was also the period of the dramatic expansion of the Church of the East along the Silk Road to China, where a famous stele, in Chinese and Syriac, dated 781, records the coming of Christianity a century and a half

---

[14] In English, there are several articles on this topic vol. 4 (2004) of the *Journal of the Canadian Society for Syriac Studies*. For the Aristotle translations, the collected articles by H. Hugonnard-Roche and J.W. Watt, mentioned in section H under Collected Volumes, are particularly important.

earlier. There is now a good general account by I. Gillman and H.-J. Klimkeit, *Christians in Asia before 1500* (Richmond, 1999). Recent new finds, and a series of conferences in Salzburg (Austria) on the topic have led to a number of new studies.[15]

The Mongol period (thirteenth to fourteenth century) is well covered in the short book by J. M. Fiey, *Chrétiens syriaques sous les Mongols* (Louvain, 1975). One of the most fascinating Syriac texts from this period is the account of the travels, from China to the Middle East and (in the case of one of them) to Western Europe, of two monks of the Church of the East (one of whom ended up as being made Patriarch!). Several English translations of this exist, the fullest is that by E. A. W. Budge, *The Monks of Kublai Khan* (London, 1928). The recent Italian translation by P. G. Borbone, *Storia di Mar Yahballaha e di Rabban Sauma* (Turin, 2000), has an excellent introduction and annotation.

The historical geography of the Syriac Churches in the area largely covered today by Iraq is the subject of several very valuable works by J. M. Fiey, above all his *Assyrie chrétienne*, I–III (Beirut, 1965–8). Father Fiey lived much of his life in Iraq and so was exceptionally well placed to write on this subject. For the period from the fourteenth to the early twentieth century (for which there are virtually no relevant narrative historical sources available) D. Wilmshurst's *The Ecclesiastical Organisation of the Church of the East* (Louvain, 2000) makes wonderful use of the evidence from colophons in over two thousand manuscripts, and is well provided with maps of villages (very appropriately the book is dedicated to the memory of Father Fiey, who died in 1995). Four detailed maps of remote villages are also to be found in J. Sanders' *Assyrian-Chaldean Christians in Eastern Turkey and Iran. Their Homeland Recharted* (Hernen, 1997).

Much information about the Church of the East in the Ottoman period, based largely on manuscript sources, is to be found in H. Murre-van den Berg, *Scribes and Scriptures. The Church of the East in the Eastern Ottoman Provinces* (Eastern Christian Studies 21; Leuven, 2015).

In the second half of the nineteenth century various western missions, mostly based in Urmia (northwestern Iran) had an important impact on the life of the Church of the East. Three books in particular cover different

---

[15] Several of these are edited by D.W. Winkler and Li Tang; volume 12 of Études syriaques (2015) is entirely devoted to the subject (for the title, see below, under H. Series. A helpful introduction to the earlier material is provided by J. Ferreira, *Early Chinese Christianity: The Tang Christian Monument and Other Documents* (Early Christian Studies 17; Strathfield NSW, 2014).

aspects of this: J. F. Coakley, *The Church of the East and the Church of England. A History of the Archbishop of Canterbury's Assyrian Mission* (Oxford, 1992); H. L. Murre-van den Berg, *From a Spoken to a Written Language. The Introduction and Development of Literary Urmia Aramaic in the Nineteenth Century* (Leiden, 1999); and (from a wider perspective) J. Joseph, *The Modern Assyrians of the Middle East. Encounters with Western Christian Missions, Archaeologists and Colonial Powers* (Leiden, 2000).[16]

A very well-informed account of developments in the twentieth century is provided by an Indian bishop of the Assyrian Church of the East, Mar Aprem, *The Assyrian Church of the East in the Twentieth Century* (Kottayam, 2003).

The West Syriac Tradition

The period of the emergence of the Syrian Orthodox Church as a separate entity, in the fifth to sixth century, is covered, from different perspectives, by W. H. C. Frend's *The Rise of the Monophysite Movement* (Cambridge, 1972) and by I. Shahid's *Byzantium and the Arabs in the Sixth Century*, I.1–2 (Washington D.C., 1995), II.1 (2002). Much more focused are F. Alpi's two volume *La route royale: Sévère d'Antioche et les Églises d'Orient (512–518)* (Beirut, 2009) and V. Menze's valuable study, *Justinian and the Making of the Syrian Orthodox Church* (Oxford, 2008). Helpful guidance to the more important theological texts of this period is now available in the course of the section "Ad Fontes" in A. Grillmeier's *Christ in Christian Tradition*, II.1 (London, 1987), and in Part III of A. van Roey and P. Allen, *Monophysite Texts of the Sixth Century* (Leuven, 1994). The obscure (and controversial!) origins of the Maronite Church which emerged as a separate body, with its own Patriarch of Antioch, in the course of the sixth and seventh centuries are objectively discussed by H. Suermann in his *Die Grundungsgeschichte der Maronitischen Kirche* (Wiesbaden, 1998). Both the Maronite and the Byzantine (or "Rum" = Rhomaios, i.e., Byzantine) Orthodox Patriarchates of Antioch accept the Council of Chalcedon and their separation from one another now clearly seems to be connected with the monothelete/dyothelete controversy of the seventh century; this is well brought out by J. Tannous in his 'In search of Monotheletism', published in *Dumbarton Oaks Papers* 68 (2014), 29–67, which makes excellent use of recently published Syriac texts which are of relevance.

---

[16] On the origins and adoption of the term 'Assyrian' there is a good study by A.H. Becker (see below, Appendix, note 23).

For the earlier Arab period the only general works available are in German: W. Hage, *Die syrisch-jakobitische Kirche in frühislamischer Zeit* (Wiesbaden, 1966), and P. Kawerau, *Die jakobitische Kirche im Zeitalter der syrischen Renaissance* (Berlin, 2nd ed. 1960); the latter deals with the twelfth to thirteenth century. A good collection of studies on the 'Syriac renaissance' is to be found in H. Teule and others (eds), *The Syriac Renaissance. A Period of Interreligious and Intercutural Dialogue* (Eastern Christian Studies 9; Leuven, 2010).

The history of the Syrian Orthodox Church in the later Middle Ages and the Ottoman period has been little studied; for the late Ottoman period, however, there is now Kh. Dinno, *Syrian Orthodox Christians in the Late Ottoman Period and Beyond* (Piscataway NJ, 2017). Information concerning the massacres of Syriac Christians, as well as of Armenians, at the time of the First World War is now becoming more available; two important books on the subject are S. de Courtois, *The Forgotten Genocide: Eastern Christians, the last Arameans* (Piscataway NJ, 2004), and D. Gaunt, *Massacres, Resistance, Protectors: Muslim-Christian Relations in Eastern Anatolia during World War I* (Piscataway NJ, 2006).

For the historical geography of the Syrian Orthodox Church, there are two very useful works by E. Honigmann, *Évéques et Évêchés Monophysites d'Asie Antérieure au VIe siècle* (Louvain, 1951), and *Le Couvent de Barsauma et le Patriarcat Jacobite d'Antioche et de Syrie* (Louvain, 1954). The early history of Tur Abdin in southeastern Turkey, an important cultural homeland of the Syrian Orthodox Church, is expertly studied by A. N. Palmer in his *Monk and Mason on the Tigris Frontier. The Early History of Tur 'Abdin* (Cambridge, 1990). (The present-day people and architecture of the area beautifully recorded in photographs by H. Hollerweger in his *Tur Abdin. Lebendiges Kulturerbe—Living Cultural Heritage—Canli Kültür Mirasi* [Linz, 1999]).

G. BIBLIOGRAPHICAL AIDS

C. Moss's *Catalogue of Syriac Printed Books and Related Literature in the British Museum* (London, 1962) provides the nearest thing available to a bibliography of Syriac studies up to about 1959; it is arranged alphabetically by author (ancient, as well as modern). For relevant printed books of the sixteenth to nineteenth centuries, a useful listing can be found in the bibliography in Nestle's *Syriac Grammar*.

From 1960 onwards reasonably complete coverage is provided by the periodic classified bibliographies published in *Parole de l'Orient* as follows:

1960–1970: *Parole de l'Orient* 4 (1973), pp. 393–465.

1971–1980: *Parole de l'Orient* 10 (1981/2), pp. 291–412.

1981–1985: *Parole de l'Orient* 14 (1987), pp. 289–360.

1986–1990: *Parole de l'Orient* 17 (1992), pp. 211–301.

These four have also been combined into a single volume: S. P. Brock, *Syriac Studies: a Classified Bibliography (1960–1990)* (Kaslik, 1996).

1991–1995: *Parole de l'Orient* 23 (1998), pp. 241–350.

1996–2000: *Parole de l'Orient* 29 (2004), pp. 263–410.

2001–2005: *Parole de l'Orient* 33 (2008), pp. 281-448.

2006–2010: *Parole de l'Orient* 38 (2013), pp. 241-452.

These four have now likewise been combined into a single volume, *Syriac Studies: a Classified Bibliography (1991–2010)* (Kaslik, 2014). The growing size of each of these bibliographies is a pleasing indication of the increasing academic interest in Syriac studies.

An annual listing of new books of Syriac relevance can be found in the first number of *Hugoye* each year (from 1998 onwards); from 2017 onwards it is planned to include articles as well (listed alphabetically by author, rather than by subject).

An excellent searchable bibliography on Syriac Christianity is also available on the internet (see Section I, below).

There are also a number of specialized bibliographies (those for the Peshitta Old Testament have already been mentioned above). The following alphabetic list combines individual authors and topics:

Ascetic and mystical literature: G. Kessel and K. Pinggéra, *A Bibliography of Syriac Ascetic and Mystical Literature* (Eastern Christian Studies, 11; Leuven, 2011).

Barhebraeus: J.M. Fiey, "Esquisse d'une bibliographie de Bar Hebraeus (+1286)," *Parole de l'Orient* 13 (1986), pp. 279–312 and especially H. Takahashi, *Barhebraeus: A Bio-Bibliography* (Piscataway NJ, 2005).

Catalogues of Manuscripts: A. Desreumaux (with F. Briquel Chatonnet), *Répertoire des bibliothèques et des catalogues de manuscrits syriaques* (Paris, 1991). Some addenda, mostly from Middle Eastern libraries, are provided by C. Detienne in *Le Muséon* 105 (1992), pp. 283–302. Several catalogues of important collections have subsequently been published, in particular: Deir al-Surian (Egypt), by S.P. Brock and L. van Rompay (2014); Paris, by F.

Briquel-Chatonnet (1997); St Catherine's Monastery, Sinai ('New Finds'): manuscripts by Mother Philothea of Sinai (2008), and fragments by S.P. Brock (1995). A number of Middle Eastern collections are now covered by the work of Hill Museum and Manuscript Library (HMML) in Collegeville, Minnesota.[17]

Ephrem: K. den Biesen, *Bibliography of Ephrem the Syrian* (Giove in Umbria, 2002; 2nd edition, 2011). Basic guidance to editions and translations of the genuine works can be found in J. Melki, "Éphrem le syrien. Un bilan de l'édition critique," *Parole de l'Orient* 11 (1983), pp. 3–88, and in my "A brief guide to the main editions and translations of the works of St Ephrem," *The Harp* 3:1/2 (1990), pp. 7–29; an expanded edition is published in *Khristianskij Vostok* 6(XII) (2013), pp. 13–77.

Inscriptions: H. J. W. Drijvers and J. F. Healey, *The Old Syriac Inscriptions of Edessa & Osrhoene* (Leiden, 1999). This collects all the inscriptions belonging to the first to third centuries, several of which are in mosaics. A bibliography of publications of inscriptions (most of which are from the fifth century or later) is given in my *Studies in Syriac Christianity* (1992), Chapter 3 (originally published in 1978; subsequent publications can readily be found in the section "Inscriptions" in the bibliographies in *Parole de l'Orient*). The inscriptions of Tur 'Abdin are collected by A. N. Palmer in *Oriens Christianus* 71 (1987), pp. 53–139. A Corpus of all known Syriac inscriptions is in the course of preparation; so far two volumes have appeared: F. Briquel-Chatonnet, A. Desreumaux, and J. Thekeparampil, *Recueil des inscriptions syriaques*, I. *Kérala* (Paris, 2008); and A. Harrak, II, *Iraq: Syriac and Garshuni Inscriptions*, I–II ((Paris, 2010). An idea of the range of the material can be seen from the chapters in *Les inscriptions syriaques*, edited by F. Briquel Chatonnet, M. Debié, and A. Desreumaux (Paris, 2004).

Isaac of Antioch: E. G. Mathews, "A bibliographical clavis to the corpus of works attributed to Isaac of Antioch," *Hugoye* 5:1 (2002), pp. 3–14, and 6:1 (2003), pp. 51–76.

Jacob of Edessa: D. Kruisheer and L. van Rompay, "A bibliographical clavis to the works of Jacob of Edessa," *Hugoye* 1:1 (1998).

---

[17] See C. Stewart, "HMML and Syriac manuscripts" in F. Briquel-Chatonnet and M. Debié (eds), *Manuscripta Syriaca* (Paris, 2015), pp. 49–63.

Jacob of Serugh: Kh. Alwan, "Bibliographie générale raisonnée de Jacques de Saroug," *Parole de l'Orient* 13 (1986), pp. 313–83, and S.P. Brock, "Jacob of Serugh: a select bibliographical guide", in G.A. Kiraz (ed.), *Jacob of Serugh and his Times* (Piscataway NJ, 2010), pp. 219–244.

Liturgy: J-M. Sauget, *Bibliographie des liturgies orientales (1900–1960)* (Rome, 1962); S. Janeras, *Bibliografia sulle liturgie orientali (1961–1967)* (Rome, 1069); P. Yousif, *A Classified Bibliography on the East Syrian Liturgy* (Rome, 1990). Also very useful are: H. Brakmann, "Zu den Liturgien des christlichen Ostens", and "Literaturberichte: der Gottesdienst der östlichen Kirchen", *Archiv für Liturgiewissenschaft* 24 (1982), pp. 377–410, and 30 (1988), pp. 303–410.

H. SERIES, PERIODICALS, ENCYCLOPEDIAS, AND COLLECTED VOLUMES

Series

Pride of place is taken here by the series *Scriptores Syri* in the *Corpus Scriptorum Christianorum Orientalium* (Corpus of Oriental Christian writers), published at Louvain since 1903; by the end of 2015 a total of 255 volumes in the Syriac series had been published. The normal format is a separate volume each for text (Estrangelo script) and translation (Latin, German, French, or English); there is also a series of *Subsidia*, and several of these are specifically on Syriac topics.

A large number of Syriac texts have also been published in the *Patrologia Orientalis*, founded by R. Graffin and for long edited by his nephew F. Graffin (d. 2002). By the end of 2015 a total of 53 volumes (in 236 fascicules) had appeared, of which 69 fascicules concern Syriac texts. In this series the translation (now normally French) either faces the text, or (in older volumes) is placed under it. R. Graffin also started another series, *Patrologia Syriaca*, of which, however, only three volumes ever appeared (not to be confused with Ortiz de Urbina's history of Syriac literature under the same title). An interesting account of R. Graffin's series is provided by L. Mariès and F. Graffin in *Orientalia Christiana Periodica* 67 (2001), pp. 157–78.

Although not in a series, the large number of Syriac writers edited by Lazarist Father Paul Bedjan (1838–1920) should not be left without mention. Between 1888 and 1910 he published over fifteen volumes (often running to well over 500 pages each), of Syriac texts, which were printed (by W. Drugulin of Leipzig) in a beautiful East Syrian script.[18] Appreciations of Bedjan's notable contribution to Syriac studies are to be found by J. M. Vosté in *Orientalia Christiana Periodica* 2 (1945), pp. 45–102, and by H. Murre-van den Berg in vol. VI of the Gorgias reprint of Jacob of Serugh's verse homilies (2006).

Many of A. Mingana's publications of Syriac (and some Garshuni [Arabic in Syriac script]) texts from the Mingana Collection of Manuscripts (Birmingham, GB) were published in the series Woodbrooke Studies. Between 1927 and 1934 seven volumes appeared, the widely known being the last, entitled *Early Christian Mystics*.

A series edited until his death (in 1996) by W. Strothmann is *Göttinger Orientforschungen, Reihe Syriaca* (35 volumes, 1971–1994). In the earlier volumes a typewriter with Estrangelo script, developed in Holland, was employed for the Syriac texts. (This is one of the three Syriac typewriter faces that seem to have been produced; another, designed some time ago in Germany, is based on the modern East Syrian script, and was employed to type the Modern Syriac texts in a collection of these by R. Macuch and E. Panoussi). The series has recently been revived, and several volumes involve Syriac topics, among them vol. 41 (2012) and 46 (2014) with the papers of the VIth and VIIth German-speaking Syrologen-Symposia.

An important series for studies on the Syriac Bible (especially the Old Testament) is to be found in the *Monographs of the Peshitta Institute, Leiden,* already mentioned above (in section D).

In Lebanon the Centre d'études et de recherches orientales (CERO) (Antelias) has organised (since 1993) an annual series of colloquia on different topics under the general title *Patrimoine syriaque*, whose proceedings are published in European languages and in Arabic (in separate volumes). Many valuable papers can be found in these, above all in the *Actes de Colloque IX: Les Syriaques transmetteurs de civilisations. l'expérience du Bilad el-Sham à l'epoque omeyyade* (2005). The first four colloquia concerned liturgical topics, the fifth and sixth dealt with Syriac monastic tradition, while the seventh and eighth were on spirituality. More recently CERO has inaugurated another series, Sources syriaques, in which is intended to publish important Syriac texts accompanied by translations; a volume to introduce the series, entitled *Nos sources. Arts et littérature syriaques* (Antelias, 2005), provides a very

---

[18] There is a fascinating history of Syriac printing, by J. F. Coakley, *The Typography of Syriac. A Historical Catalogue of Printing Types, 1537–1958* (London/ New Castle, Delaware, 2006).

useful introduction to different genres of Syriac literature, contributed by both Middle Eastern and Western scholars.

It is a gratifying sign of the increasingly wide interest in the Syriac tradition that in different countries or regions there are now regular series of conferences. The earliest was in Kerala (India), organized by the St Ephrem Ecumenical Research Institute (SEERI; see below under Periodicals), followed by North America (1991), Germany (1998), Canada (2000), Italy (2002), and France (2003); some of the publications resulting from these are mentioned below.

Beginning in 2002 the Centro Ambrosiano in Milan has had a series of conferences on the Syriac tradition; six volumes (2003–2012), edited by E. Vergani and S. Chialà, containing the papers from these meetings have been published. With the establishment of a Syriac section in the Accademia Ambrosiana, papers have been published in *Orientalia Ambrosiana* 1– (2012–).

Since 2004 the French Societé des études syriaques (Paris) has published voumes on specific topics based on their annual meetings. These volumes provide an excellent way in to scholarship in a particular area of Syriac studies:

1. *Les inscriptions syriaques* (2004).
2. *Les apocrypes syriaques* (2005)
3. *Les liturgies syriaques* (2006).
4. *Les Pères grecs dans la tradition syriaque* (2007).
5. *L'Ancien Testament en syriaque* (2008).
6. *L'historiographie syriaque* (2009).
7. *Le monachisme syriaque* (2010).
8. *Les mystiques syriaques* (2011).
9. *L'hagiographie syriaque* (2011).
10. *Les églises en monde syriaque* (2012).
11. *Les sciences en syriaque* (2013)
12. *Le christianisme syriaque en Asie centrale et en Chine* (2015).
13. *Les controverses religieuses em syriaque* (2016).
14. *Le Nouveau Testamemt en syriaque* (2017, forthcoming).

Modern technology has greatly facilitated the production of bilingual editions, with text and translation on facing pages. Gorgias Press has several series, notably for the Persian Martyrdoms and for Jacob of Serugh's Verse Homilies. The broader series of Texts from Christian Late Antiquity also contains several volumes of works by Syriac authors. Another bilingual series is Eastern Christian Texts, published by Brigham Young University

(Provo, Utah); of the several volumes published so far, one involves a Syriac author: S.P. Brock and G.A. Kiraz, *Ephrem the Syrian: Select Poems* (2006).

There are also some wider series which often include volumes of specifically Syriac interest, notably:

Eastern Christian Studies (Leuven): among the relevant volumes is number 20 (2015), entitled *Syriac Encounters*, contains the papers from the Sixth North Ameican Syriac Symposium.

Orientalia – Patristica – Oecumenica (Münster).

Studien zur Orientalischen Kirchengeschichte (Münster), is edited by M. Tamcke and others. Several volumes are of Syriac interest, in particular those publishing the papers from some of the Deutsche Syrologen-Symposia: *Syriaca [I]* constitutes vol. 17 (2002), and *Syriaca II* vol. 33 (2004).

Finally, mention should be made of a series of monographs in Arabic, entitled *Syriac Patrimony*, and edited by Mor Gregorios Yohanna Ibrahim, Syrian Orthodox Metropolitan of Aleppo. The series includes a number of very useful volumes, in particular nos. 8–10, which are editions of detailed catalogues of Syriac manuscripts in various Syrian Orthodox libraries made by Mor Filoksinos Yohanna Dolabani and reproduced from his handwriting. An idea of the series can be gained from the review A. N. Palmer in *Parole de l'Orient* 23 (1998), pp. 217–231. Mor Gregorios was kidnapped by unknown persons on 22nd April 2013, and his fate, and that of his companion, Mor Paul Yazigi, Rum Orthodox Metropolitan of Aleppo who was kidnapped with him, remains unknown. A volume of tributes to Mor Gregorios was published in 2016.

Periodicals

In the past Syriac studies have rarely had a periodical devoted solely to themselves, though now the field is rather better provided for, notably by the Internet *Hugoye*, *The Harp*, and the *Journal of the Canadian Society for Syriac Studies*. The following list also covers the chief periodicals where Syriac texts and articles of Syriac interest are frequently published (the list is alphabetical):

- *Analecta Bollandiana.* This specializes in hagiographical texts (in any language) and it is published by the venerable and learned Society of Bollandists in Brussels.

- *Aram.* This is the publication of the Aram Society for Syro-Mesopotamian Studies (founded and directed by Fr. Shafiq

Abouzayd, a Maronite priest with a doctorate from Fribourg in Switzerland who looks after the Melkite parish in London). The Aram Society holds annual conferences in Oxford (and occasionally elsewhere) which attract scholars from the Middle East as well as from Europe and America; for the most part the volumes contain the conference papers.

- *Collectanea Christiana Orientalia* (2004–). This new periodical, published in Córdoba, Spain, is edited jointly from the Facultad de Filosofia y Letras of the Universidad de Córdoba and the Centre de documentation et de recherches Arabes Chrétiennes (CEDRAC) of the Université Saint-Joseph, Beirut. Although most articles so far have been in the field of Christian Arabic, articles on aspects of Syriac studies are sometimes also included.

- *The Harp: A Review of Syriac and Oriental Studies.* This has been published since 1987 by the St. Ephrem Ecumenical Research Institute (SEERI), in Kottayam (Kerala, India), which had been inaugurated in 1985, and is now a research institute affiliated to the Mahatma Gandhi University of Kottayam. Fr. Jacob Thekeparampil (its founder and present Director) had spent several years in Europe, first doing his doctorate in Paris and then continuing in Göttingen; during this time he collected the basis of SEERI's remarkably fine specialist library on Syriac studies. Besides teaching M.A. and other courses, SEERI organises international Syriac conferences once every four years, and several numbers of *The Harp* contain papers from these. An index, compiled by M. Hansbury, to the first 25 issues of *The Harp* is to be found in vol. 26 (2012), pp. 1–131. SEERI also publishes two monograph series, one in English, entitled *Moran Etho* (several of which have subsequently been republished by the Gorgias Press), and the other in Malayalam. SEERI has also published a correspondence course on the Syrian Christian Heritage.

- *Hugoye: Journal of Syriac Studies* (http://bethmardutho.org/index.php/hugoye/about-hugoye.html). This is the journal of Beth Mardutho: The Syriac Institute, founded by George Kiraz in 1992 (http://www.bethmardutho.org). Besides other things Beth Mardutho has developed different Syriac computer fonts, and was behind the inclusion of Syriac among the unicode scripts. *Hugoye* has been published on the internet twice yearly since 1998; volumes for each year are now also be available in printed form as well. An index for vols. 1–10, by J. Walters, has been published separately (Piscataway NJ, 2011).

- *Journal of Assyrian Academic Studies.* This is the academic successor of the *Journal of the Assyrian Academic Society* (from vol. 11 (1997)); although the focus is more on Modern Syriac and related issues, there are also quite a number of articles on Classical Syriac topics.

- *Journal of the Canadian Society for Syriac Studies.* This useful annual has been edited from the University of Toronto (by Professor A. Harrak) from 2001 onwards. Many of the contributions have their origin in papers by international scholars given at meetings of the Society.

- *Journal of Eastern Christian Studies.* This is the new English-title continuation of *Het christlelijk Oosten*, published by the Institute of Eastern Christian Studies, Nijmegen. Volume 56 (2004) contains the main papers from the Eighth Symposium Syriacum, held in Sydney, Australia in 2000.

- *Journal/Bulletin of the Syriac Academy Baghdad.* The Syriac Academy was established in Baghdad shortly after the Iraqi Government had proclaimed Syriac to be a recognized cultural language of the country (decree of 22 April, 1972). Although most articles are in Arabic (with English summaries), a few numbers have a short English section with contributions by Western scholars. Volumes 2 and 3 contain particularly important collections of Syriac inscriptions in Iraq (P. Haddad). Needless to say publication in recent years has been very difficult (and often impossible); volume 17 came out in 1999.

- *Le Muséon.* Many numbers contain publications of shorter Syriac texts. There are now two separate index volumes; these cover all the numbers from its inception (1882) up to 1931, and thence to 1973.

- *Oriens Christianus.* This august periodical has been published since 1901 and for a long time it was edited by A. Baumstark.

The immensely useful *Gesamtregister für die Bände 1 (1901) bis 70 (1986)* (Wiesbaden, 1989) was compiled by the present editor, H. Kaufhold; besides various indexes (including manuscripts cited), this also lists the contents of each number.

- *Orientalia Christiana Periodica.* This is published by the Pontifical Oriental Institute in Rome. An index for volumes 26–50 (1960–1984) is provided in *OCP* 52 (1986). There is a separate series of monographs under the title *Orientalia Christiana Analecta* in which volumes 197 (1974), 205 (1978), 221 (1983), 229 (1987), 236 (1990), 247 (1994), and 256 (1998) contain the papers given at the international Symposia Syriaca, I–VII (VIII has been published in *Journal of Eastern Christian Studies* 56 [2004]; IX, X and XI in *Parole de l'Orient*, for which see below).

- *Orientalia Lovaniensia Periodica.* This has been published since 1970 by the Flemish-speaking Department of Oriental Studies at Leuven (Louvain); articles are in English, French, and German. There is also a monograph series, *Orientalia Lovaniensia Analecta*, which has several volumes containing material of Syriac interest.

- *L'Orient Syrien.* Full of informative articles, this was edited from 1956 until 1967, shortly before his death, by Mgr. Gabriel Khouri-Sarkis, Syrian Catholic Chorepiscopus living in Paris. The contributions (all in French) are generally excellent examples of "haute vulgarisation," and include many translations of Syriac texts. There is an index in the *Mémorial Mgr. G. Khouri-Sarkis* (Louvain, 1969).

- *Parole de l'Orient.* This important periodical is published by the Maronite Université Saint Esprit at Kaslik in Lebanon; articles are usually in French and at first the majority dealt with Syriac topics, though in recent years Christian Arabic has sometimes predominated. The first number of *Parole de l'Orient* (or, to use its Syriac title, *Melto d-Madnho*) appeared in 1970 as a successor to *Melto: Recherches orientales*, which ran between 1965 and 1969. There is an index to both *Melto* and *Parole de l'Orient*, covering from 1965 to 1998, in *Parole de l'Orient* 23 (1998), pp. 359–403. Papers from the international Symposia Syriaca IX–XI are published in volumes 31, 33, 35, 36, 38 and 40 (2006–2015).

- *Revue de l'Orient Chrétien*. This valuable periodical, edited by R. Graffin, ran from 1896 to 1946; there are indices at the end of every ten volumes.

- *The Syrian Orthodox Patriarchal Magazine*. Especially in recent years this long-established periodical has included important studies in English as well as Arabic.

Needless to say, articles on Syriac topics appear sporadically in many other periodicals as well.

Encyclopedias

The *Gorgias Encyclopedic Dictionary of the Syriac Heritage* (ed. S.P. Brock, A. Butts, G.A. Kiraz, and L. van Rompay; Piscataway NJ, 2011) now provides a single-volume encyclopedia devoted specifically to Syriac studies. All main Syriac authors and select topics are covered, and each entry contains a basic bibliography; illustrations and maps are also provided. A number of other encyclopedias and dictionaries, which have a different scope, include some coverage of the Syriac tradition; these include the following:

- *The Blackwell Dictionary of Eastern Christianity* (ed. K. Parry, D. J. Melling, D. Brady, S. H. Griffith, and J. F. Healey; Oxford, 1999).

- *Dictionnaire d'histoire et de géographie ecclésiastiques* (Paris, 1912–). This has only reached the middle of the letter L (vol. 31) by the end of 2015. Syriac is rather well covered (both persons and places).

- *Dictionnaire de Spiritualité* (Paris, 1932–95; 17 volumes). There are several excellent and important contributions of relevance (e.g., on Ephrem and Isaac of Niniveh).

- *Dizionario enciclopedico dell'Oriente cristiano* (ed. E. G. Farrugia, Rome, 2000), with new English edition, *Encyclopedic Dictionary of the Christian East* (Rome, 2015). A useful one-volume reference work covering the whole of the Christian East.

- *Encyclopaedia Iranica* (New York, 1985–). This contains several substantial articles of relevance. It has reached the letter K (vol. 16) by the end of 2015.

- *Encyclopedia of Ancient Christianity* (ed. A. di Berardino and others; in 3 volumes, Downers Grove, Illinois, 2014). This is based on A. di Berardino's *Nuovo dizionario patristico e di antichità Cristiana*, the update of the next item. An excellent and very useful resource.

- *Encyclopedia of the Early Church* (ed. A. di Berardino; English tr. Cambridge, 1992), in two volumes, with good Syriac coverage. For the new edition, see the previous item.

- *Encyclopedia of Early Christianity* (ed. E. Ferguson; New York, 2nd ed. 1997), in two volumes, with quite good Syriac coverage.

- *Encyclopédie maronite* (Kaslik). Only the first volume (1992) has appeared so far, covering A (thus one can sort out the numerous Assemanis).

- *Kleines Wörterbuch des christlichen Orient* (ed. J. Assfalg and P. Krüger; Wiesbaden, 1975; enlarged 2nd edn, 2007); there is a French translation, *Petit dictionnaire de l'Orient chrétien* (Turnhout, 1991).

- *Lexikon der antiken christlichen Literatur* (ed. S. Döpp and W. Geerlings, Freiburg, 1998). This handy single-volume work has good coverage of Syriac writers.

- *Lexikon für Theologie und Kirche* (3rd ed., Freiburg, 1993–2001; 11 volumes). Syriac authors are rather well covered, though the entries are usually brief.

- *The Oxford Dictionary of the Christian Church* (3rd revised ed., ed. E. A. Livingstone; Oxford, 2005).

- *The Oxford Dictionary of Late Antiquity*, ed. O. Nicholson (Oxford, 2018 [forthcoming]). Syriac topics are well covered.

- *The Oxford Handbook of Late Antiquity*, ed. S.F. Johnson (Oxford, 2012). Syriac topics are well covered.

- *Religion in Geschichte und Gegenwart* (4th ed., 1998–2005), with English translation, *Religion Past and Present* (Leiden, 2005–2013. Only main Syriac names and topics are covered, but with detailed articles.

- *Theologische Realenzyklopädie* (1976–2007). Likewise only main names and topics, but entries are detailed.

For the Syriac Bible, helpful articles can be found, for example, in *The Anchor Dictionary of the Bible* (1992).

Although plans for a *Bibliotheca Hagiographica Syriaca* were announced in *Aram* 5 (1993), it now seems unlikely that this will materialize as originally planned, so recourse must still be made to P. Peeters, *Bibliotheca Hagiographica Orientalis* of 1910.[19] The situation is to some extent remedied by J. M. Fiey's *Les saints syriaques* (Princeton NJ, 2004), a work which he had completed shortly before he died in 1995; this is in the form of a dictionary of saints. Some of Fiey's material for this work was used for the *Enciclopedia dei Santi. Le Chiese orientali*, I–II (Rome, 1998–9).

Another most valuable reference work produced by Fiey towards the end of his life was *Pour un Oriens Christianus Novus. Répertoire des diocèses syriaques orientaux et occidentaux* (Beirut/Stuttgart, 1993). By his title Fr. Fiey (who was a Dominican) deliberately reflected that of the magisterial three-volume *Oriens Christianus*, compiled by his fellow Dominican, Michel Le Quien, which was published posthumously in 1740 (photographic reprint, Graz, 1958). Le Quien's work covered all the Eastern Churches, whereas Fiey confines himself to the Church of the East (with the Chaldean Catholic Church) and the Syrian Orthodox (and Catholic) Church. Its modern equivalent, with good coverage for the Syriac Churches, is G. Fedalto, *Hierarchi Ecclesiastica Orientalis*, II (Padua, 1988).

For the subject of Law there is an authoritative introductory account by H. Kaufhold, "Sources of Canon Law in the Eastern Churches", in W. Hartman and K. Pennington (eds), *The History of Byzantine and Eastern Canon Law to 1500* (Washington DC, 2012), pp. 215–342.

Collected volumes

Festschriften (the bane of librarians), memorial volumes, and other collections may sometimes be devoted entirely, or largely to Syriac studies. The following list, alphabeticized under the name of the scholar concerned, is confined to works which are wholly, or primarily, of Syriac concern. Many Festschriften include a bibliography of the scholar being honoured.

Mar Aprem, (Festschrift): = *The Harp* 15 (2002).

---

[19] For the contents, with some updating, see the Annotated bibliography of Syriac Resources Online, http://www.syri.ac. under Hagiography (also section I, below).

J. Assfalg, (Festschrift): ed. R. Schulz and M. Görg, *Festgabe für Julius Assfalg* (Ägypten und Altes Testament 20; 1990). There is an index in *Oriens Christianus* 76 (1992), pp. 275–9.

S. P. Brock, *Syriac Perspectives on Late Antiquity* (Variorum Reprints, London, 1984).

_____, *Studies in Syriac Christianity* (Variorum Reprints, Aldershot, 1992).

_____, *From Ephrem to Romanos. Interactions between Syriac and Greek in Late Antiquity* (Variorum Reprints, Aldershot, 1999).

_____, *Fire from Heaven: Studies in Syriac Theology and Liturgy* (Variorum Reprints, Aldershot, 2006).

_____, (Festschrift): = *Aram* 5 (1993).

_____, (Festschrift): ed. G.A. Kiraz, *Malphono w-rabo d-malphone. Studies in Honour of Sebastian P. Brock* (Piscataway, 2008).

J.F. Coakley, (Festschrift): = *Journal of Assyrian Academic Studies* 21:2 (2007).

A. Desreumaux, (Festschrift): ed. F. Briquel-Chatonnet and M. Debié, *Sur les pas des Araméens chrétiens. Mélanges offerts à Alain Desreumaux* (Paris, 2010).

H. J. W. Drijvers, *East of Antioch. Studies in Early Syriac Christianity* (Variorum Reprints, London, 1984).

_____, *History and Religion in Late Antique Syria* (Variorum Reprints, Aldershot, 1994).

_____, (Festschrift): ed. G. J. Reinink and A. C. Klugkist, *After Bardaisan. Studies on Continuity and Change in Syriac Christianity in Honour of Professor Han J. W. Drijvers* (Orientalia Lovaniensia Analecta 89, 1999).

_____, (Festschrift): ed. H. L.J. Vanstiphout, *All those Nations. Cultural Encounters within and with the Near East. Studies presented to Han Drijvers* (Groningen, 1999).

J. M. Fiey, *Communautés syriaques en Iran et Iraq des origines à 1552* (Variorum Reprints, London, 1979).

_____, (Memorial volume): *In Memoriam Professeur Jean Maurice Fiey (1914–1995)* (Annales du Département des Lettres Arabes, Université Saint-Joseph, 6-B, 1991/2 [1996]).

S. Gerö, (Festschrift): ed. D. Bumazhov, E. Grypeou, T.B. Sailors, and A. Topel, *Bibel, Byzanz und christlicher Orient. Festschrift für S. Gerö* (Orientalia Lovaniensia Analecta 187; 2011)

F. Graffin, (Festschrift): = *Parole de l'Orient* 6/7 (1975/6).

S.H. Griffiith, (Festschrift): ed. R. Darling Young and M.J. Blanchard, *To Train his Soul in Books. Asceticism in Early Christianity* (Washington DC, 2011).

A. Guillaumont, (Festschrift): ed. R-G. Coquin and E. Lucchesi, *Mélanges Antoine Guillaumont: Contributions à l'étude des christianismes orientaux* (Cahiers d'Orientalisme, Geneva, 1988).

_____, (Memorial): eds F. Jullien and M-J. Pierre, *Monachismes d'Orient. Images, échanges, influences. Hommage à Antoine Guillaumont* (Turnhout, 2011).

W. Hage, (Festschrift): ed. M. Tamcke, W. Schwaigert, and E. Schlarb, *Syrisches Christentum weltweit. Studien zur syrischen Kirchengeschichte. Festschrift für Wolfgang Hage* (Studien zur Orientalischen Kirchengeschichte 1, 1995).

M. Hayek, (Festschrift): ed. C. Chartouni, *Christianisme oriental. Kérugma et histoire. Mélanges offerts au Père Michel Hayek* (Paris, 2007).

H. Hugonnard-Roche, *La logique d'Aristote du grec au syriaque. Études sur la transmission des textes de l'Organon et leur interprétation philosophique* (Paris, 2004).

_____, (Festschrift): ed. E. Coda amd C. Martini Bonadeo, *De l'Antiquite tardive au Moyen Âge. Études de logique aristotélicienne et de philosophie grecque, syriaque, arabe et latine offertes à Henri Hugonnard-Roche* (Paris, 2014).

K.D. Jenner, (Festschrift): ed. W. Th. Van Peursen and R. B. ter Haar Romeny, *Text, Translation and Tradition. Studies on the Peshitta and its Use in the Syriac Tradition presented to Konrad D. Jenner* (Monographs of the Peshitta Institute 14; Leiden, 2006).

H. Kaufhold, (Festschrift): ed. P. Bruns and H.O. Luthe, *Orientalia Christiana. Festschrift für Hubert Kaufhold* (Wiesbaden, 2013).

G. Khouri-Sarkis, (Memorial volume): ed. F. Graffin, *Mémorial Mgr Gabriel Khouri- Sarkis (1898–1968)* (Louvain, 1969).

G. Paniker, (Festschrift): = *The Harp* 16 (2003).

G. Reinink, *Syriac Christianity under Late Sasanian and Early Islamic Rule* (Variorum Reprints, 2005).

————, (Festschrift): ed. W.J. van Bekkum, J.W. Drijvers, and A.C. Klugkist, *Syriac Polemics. Studies in Honour of Gerrit Jan Reinink* (Orientlaia Lovaniensia Analecta 170; 2007).

J. M. Sauget (ed. L. Duval-Arnould and F. Rilliet), *Littératures et manuscrits des chrétientés syriaques et arabes. Receuil des articles* (Studi e Testi 389, 1998).

W. Strothmann, (Festschrift): ed. G. Wiessner, *Erkenntnisse und Meinungen,* II (Göttinger Orientforschungen, Reihe Syriaca 17, 1978).

M. Tamcke, (Festschrift): ed. S.H. Griffith and S. Grebenstein, *Christsein in der islamischen Welt. Festschrift für Martin Tamcke* (Wiesbaden, 2015).

J. Thekeparampil, (Festschrift): = *The Harp* 20 (2006).

M. van Esbroeck, (Memorial volume): ed. V. Lourie, in *Scrinium* (St. Petersburg) 2 (2006).

A. Vööbus, (Festschrift): ed. R. H. Fischer, *A Tribute to Arthur Vööbus* (Chicago, 1977).

J.W. Watt, *Rhetoric and Philosophy from Greek into Syriac* (Variorum Reprints, 2010).

Finally in this section mention should be made of the Gorgias Press, which specializes in publications of Syriac interest (www.gorgiaspress.com). It will no doubt have been noticed that a considerable number of books cited earlier have been published in Piscataway NJ: this is the home of the Gorgias Press, founded and directed by George Kiraz. One of the great services of the Gorgias Press has been the reprinting of essential tools for Syriac studies, such as J. S. Assemani's *Bibliotheca Orientalis,* W. Wright's *Catalogue of Syriac Manuscripts in the British Museum,* and W. P. Hatch's *Album of Dated Syriac Manuscripts* (with an additional introduction by L. van Rompay); likewise the Gorgias Press has reprinted a large number of editions of Syriac texts, sometimes with added Prefaces, or even added materials (as in the case of Bedjan's edition of Jacob of Serugh's verse homilies).

George Kiraz is also the founder of Beth Mardutho: The Syriac Institute, already mentioned above (under *Hugoye*) in the section on Periodicals. One of Beth Mardutho's current projects has been the digitization of all publications of Syriac relevance that are out of copyright, the aim being to provide a library of Syriac studies that is readily accessible to everyone. Since even the best university libraries usually have serious gaps in their holdings in this field, this virtual library will be of immense value for Syriac studies in the future.

A set of volumes most easily acquired through Gorgias Press, though not published by it, is entitled *The Hidden Pearl. The Syrian Orthodox Church and its Ancient Aramaic Heritage* (3 illustrated volumes and 3 documentaries). Although the title suggests that the work might solely be of interest to the Syrian Orthodox, in fact it is only a few chapters in the third volume which deal specifically with that Church; all the other chapters are of interest for the Syriac tradition as a whole, as will be clear from the list of contents:

Vol. I. *The Ancient Aramaic Heritage* (by S.P. Brock and D.G.K. Taylor):

1. Introduction; 2. Aramaic among the languages of the Middle East; 3. The Aramaic scripts and the history of the alphabet; 4. The Aramaic Kingdoms; 5. Religion and Culture; 6. Aramaic as the official language of the Achaemenid empire; 7. The aftermath of Alexander's conquests; 8. Relics of Aramaic literature from the first millennium BC.

Vol. II. *The Heirs of the Ancient Aramaic Heritage* (by E. Balicka-Witakowski, S.P. Brock, D.G.K. Taylor and W. Witakowski):

1. Introduction; 2. Aramaic in Palestine at the time of Jesus and in the early centuries of Christianity; 3. Let the inscriptions speak: the evidence of Jewish Aramaic and Christian Syriac, fourth to seventh century; 4. The flowering of the Aramaic literatures (Jewish, Samaritan, Mandaean, Manichaean, Christian Palestinian, and Syriac); 5. The Syriac Christian traditon; 6. The spread of Syriac Christianity; 7. The Arts: architecture, wall painting and manuscript illustration; 8. The art of the scribe.

Vol. III. *At the Turn of the Third Millennium: the Syrian Orthodox Witness* (by S.P. Brock and W. Witakowski):

1. Introduction: the modern heirs of the Aramaic heritage; 2. The Churches of the Syriac tradition; 3. The Syrian Orthodox people in the

twentieth century; 4. The Syrian Orthodox presence worldwide; 5. The people and their language: cultivating Syriac; 6. Twentieth-century writing in Syriac; 7. The wider significance of the Syriac tradition; 8. In retrospect: a glance back to the past (Syriac historical writing; a mini-dictionary of Syriac authors, third to twentienth century); 9. The Bible in Syriac.

Since the volumes deliberately avoided any footnotes, the basic annotation that scholars are likely to want is provided separately, in *Hugoye* 5:1 (2002), pp. 63–112.

I. ONLINE RESOURCES FOR SYRIAC STUDIES

Prepared by J. Edward Walters

In 2012, Kristian Heal published an article that began the process of compiling online resources for the study of Syriac: K. Heal, "Corpora, eLibraries and Databases: locating Syriac Studies in the 21st century", *Hugoye* 15:1 (2012), pp. 65–78.[20] This list builds upon Kristian's important work.

Bibliographies

Comprehensive Bibliography on Syriac Christianity
    http://www.csc.org.il/db/db.aspx?db=SB

Syri.ac: An Annotated Bibliography of Syriac Resources Online
    http://syri.ac

Databases

Syriaca.org: The Syriac Reference Portal
    http://syriaca.org

Syriaca.org presently has a series of tools available that can be broken down further into more specific categories:

Geography

The Syriac Gazetteer:
    http://syriaca.org/geo/index.html

---

[20] Available at: http://www.bethmardutho.org/index.php/hugoye/volume-index/505.html

People

A Guide to Syriac Authors:
    http://syriaca.org/authors/index.html

Qadishe: Guide to the Syriac Saints:
    http://syriaca.org/q/index.html

Hagiography

Gateway to the Syriac Saints:
    http://syriaca.org/saints/index.html

Bibliotheca Hagiographica Syriaca Electronica:
    http://syriaca.org/saints/index.html

Texts / Corpora

Comprehensive Aramaic Lexicon:
    http://cal1.cn.huc.edu/

Oxford-BYU Corpus:
    https://www.syriaccorpus.org

Syriac Library (maintained by Roger Pearse):
    http://www.tertullian.org/rpearse/thesyriaclibrary/

Manuscripts

syri.ac Manuscript Catalogs
    http://syri.ac/manuscripts

Hill Museum and Manuscript Library
    http://www.hmml.org/catalog/
    http://www.vhmml.org

e-Corpus (includes the Syriac mss at St Catherine's Monastery, Sinai, which were microfilmed by the Library of Congress in 1950)
    http://www.e-corpus.org

St. Catherine's Monastery (Library of Congress)
    https://www.loc.gov/collections/manuscripts-in-st-catherines-monastery-mount-sinai/

Sinai Palimpsests
    http://www.sinaipalimpsests.org

Database on Syriac manuscripts (Paris and other French libraries, Charfet, Florence)
    http://www.mss-syriaques.org

Mingana Collection (select Syriac manuscripts)
    http://vmr.bham.ac.uk/Collections/Mingana/part/Syriac/

Miscellaneous manuscripts, maintained by Steven Ring
    http://www.syriac.talktalk.net/On-line-Syriac-MSS.html

The World Digital Library (search for "Syriac" in their collection)
    https://www.wdl.org/en/

Vatican Digitized Syriac Manuscripts
    http://www.mss.vatlib.it/guii/scan/link1.jsp?fond=Vat.sir.

Lexica

Comprehensive Aramaic Lexicon:
    http://cal1.cn.huc.edu/

Dukhrana Multiple Lexicon Search:
    http://dukhrana.com/lexicon/search.php

SEDRA (Syriac Electronic Data Research Archive)
    sedra.bethmardutho.org

Online *Compendious Syriac Dictionary*
    http://www.tyndalearchive.com/TABS/PayneSmith/index.htm

Books

eBethArkè: The Syriac Digital Library
    http://www.bethmardutho.org/library/ebetharke

Syriac Studies Reference Library (BYU)
    https://lib.byu.edu/collections/syriac-studies-reference-library/

The Goussen collection of books on the Christian Orient
   http://digitale-sammlungen.ulb.uni-bonn.de/topic/titles/17267

Journals

Hugoye: Journal of Syriac Studies
   http://bethmardutho.org/index.php/hugoye/about-hugoye.html

Parole de l'Orient
   http://documents.irevues.inist.fr/handle/2042/34760

Fonts

Beth Mardutho Meltho fonts
   http://www.bethmardutho.org/index.php/resources/fonts.html

Other

Syriac tools and resources
   http://scrollandscreen.com/syriac/index.htm

Syriac Orthodox Resources (with a useful list of links to sites of other
Churches of Syriac tradition, as well as to some academic sites).
   http://sor.cua.edu

J. SYRIAC STUDIES, PAST AND PRESENT

Although the Council of Vienne (in France), held in 1311/12), specified
that Syriac (then called 'Chaldean') should be taught at four universities in
Europe, namely Bologna, Oxford, Paris, and Salamanca, the serious study
of Syriac by a small number of European scholars only started in the
sixteenth century. These early scholars usually learnt the language from
Maronites, for whom the Maronite College was subsequently founded in
Rome (1584). It was, however, with the help of a Syrian Orthodox priest,
Moses of Mardin, that Johann Albrecht Widmanstetter was able to publish
the first printed edition of the New Testament in Syriac (Vienna, 1555). As
the individual books went to the printers Moses provided colophons with
details concerning the work, which can now readily accessible in the
Gorgias photographic reprint of the book. The background and the story
behind the publication is well told by R. Wilkinson in his *Orientalism,
Aramaic and Kabbalah in the Catholic Reformation: the First Printing of the Syriac
New Testament* (Leiden, 2007).

In the following two centuries Maronite scholars continued to play an important role in Europe. Thus the first serious printed grammar of Syriac was the work of J. Amira (1596), and it was another Maronite scholar who assisted with the Syriac texts of the Paris polyglot Bible (1629–45). In the first half of the eighteenth century a number of scholars from the Assemani family played an important role, none more so than Joseph Simon Assemani, whose massive four-volume *Bibliotheca Orientalis Clementino-Vaticana* (1719–28) has already been noted, as the first serious history of Syriac literature. Much of his work was based on manucripts recently acquired by the Vatican Library from the Monastery of the Syrians (Deir al-Surian) in Egypt; although the monastery was by then entirely Coptic Orthodox, from the ninth to the early seventeenth century it had also had Syrian Orthodox monks who had built up a magnificent collection of manuscripts (see further, Chapter VI).

Although the seventeenth and eighteenth centuries witnessed a number of fine European scholars of Syriac, and some important editions of biblical books, it was not until the second half of the nineteenth century that European (and North American) Syriac scholarship really took off. This was in large part due to the stimulus and challenge provided by the large collection of early Syriac manuscripts purchased by the British Museum from Deir al-Surian. Publications of important new Syriac texts and translations from Greek started appearing almost at once; this was long before W. Wright's superb *Catalogue* of 1870–72. No longer was there any further need for the complaint, added by one medieval scribe, 'We books are many, but there is no one who reads us: what a pity that we remain unused!'

The second half of the nineteenth century witnessed the work of some of the giants of Syriac studies, whose names remain very familiar to every Syriacist today, G. Bickell, W. Cureton, P. de Lagarde, R. Duval, I. Guidi, T. Lamy, J.P.N. Land, Th. Nöldeke, R. Payne Smith, E. Sachau, and W. Wright, to name but the most prominent.

1895 saw the publication of the first edition of C. Brockelmann's *Lexicon Syriacum* (he was aged only 27 at the time!). This was the time when the riches of the Syriac collection of St Catherine's Monastery, Sinai, were beginning to come known, thanks in large part to the energy and efforts of the autodidact twin sisters, Agnes Lewis and Margaret Gibson (nées Smith). Something of the excitement of the time can be gathered from J. Soskice's *Sisters of Sinai. How Two Lady Adventurers found the Hidden Gospels* (London, 2009).

The early years of the twentieth century saw the founding of the two great series of text editions, the Patrologia Orientalis and the Corpus Scriptorum Christianorum Orientalium, as well as of the periodical *Oriens*

Christianus. Famous names of this period include A. Baumstark (whose fundamental *Geschichte der syrischen Literatur* came out in 1922), E.W. Brooks, E.A.W. Budge, F.C. Burkitt, J.B. Chabot, G. Furlani, R. Graffin and F. Nau. To these European scholars a number of Middle Eastern scholars should be added. Best known to western scholarship are Paul Bedjan (d. 1920), a tireless editor of Syriac texts, and Alphonse Mingana (d. 1937) who, financed by the philanthopist Edward Cadbury, built up the Mingana Collection of Manuscripts in Birmingham (GB), editing a number of its important new texts in Woodbrooke Studies, and providing the three-volume *Catalogue* of the Syriac manuscripts (1933–1939). Less known, except to a few specialists, are Addai Scher, Chaldean bishop of Siirt, editor of several texts in the Patrologia Orientalis, who was martyred during the massacres of 1915, the Syrian Catholic Patriarch Ignatius Ephrem Rahmani (d. 1929), liturgist and editor of Studia Syriaca, a series that published a number of rare texts, and his younger Syrian Orthodox counterpart, Patriarch Ignatius Aphram Barsaum (d. 1957), author of *The Scattered Pearls* (for which see above, under E).

The Second World War and its aftermath saw something of a lull in Syriac studies, but from the late 1950s onwards there has been an increasing stream of publications of editions and studies. Thus, over the course of twenty years from 1955 Edmund Beck, a Benedictine monk of Metten Abbey, provided much-needed new editions of all Ephrem's genuine hymns. These reliable new editions, along with the recovery of about two thirds of the original Syriac text of the Commentary on the Diatessaon attributed to Ephrem, have led to a reassessment of Ephrem and other early Syriac writers, exemplified in Robert Murray's *Symbols of Chruch and Kingdom. A Study of Early Syriac Tradition* (Cambridge, 1975; reprinted with a new foreword, Piscataway NJ, 2004).

Especially from the late 1970s onwards there have been two important new developments. As a student in the late 1950s and beginning of the 1960s I was given no awareness of any connection between western Syriac scholarship and Syriac scholars working within the different Syriac Churches. Only in the late 1970s and the 1980s did this begin to change. In part this could be attributable to the large number of immigrants to Europe of people from the various Churches of Syriac tradition, leading to a greater awareness, on the part of Europeans, of their very existence, but much more important was contact with Middle Eastern scholars such as Pierre Yousif (in Paris) and Yusuf Habbi (in Baghdad), whose work became familiar to western scholars, both through their writing and through conferences. Today happily such contact is no longer remarkable, and the dichotomy between western and Middle Eastern Syriac scholarship is a thing of the past.

The second development can be seen as having taken its origin in Peter Brown's *The World of Late Antiquity* (1971): here, for once, was a historian of the Late Roman Empire who looked beyond the sources in Greek and Latin to those in other lanuguages, including Syriac. Thanks to the influence of his writing and teaching, it is now unthinkable that anyone should study the period of Late Antiquity (now seen as extending into the early centuries of Islam and Arab rule) without paying attention to sources in the main languages of the Christian Orient.

From the latter part of the twentieth century six names might be singled out, André de Halleux, author of a magisterial study on Philoxenus of Mabbug and editor of many of his writings, René Draguet, editor of the CSCO and contributor to it of many volumes, Jean-Maurice Fiey, whose topographical histories, in his *Assyrie chrétienne* and elsewhere, will long remain fundamental, François Graffin, editor and contributor to numerous volumes of the Patrologia Orientalis, Werner Strothmann, tireless promoter of Syriac studies in Germany and editor of many volumes in the Syriac series of Göttinger Orientforschungen, Arthur Vööbus who, despite losing his library twice to invading armies, contributed hugely to Syriac studies with his three-volume *History of Asceticism in the Syrian Orient* and his many editions, often introducing western scholars to manuscripts and texts of the Middle East of which they had hitherto been totally unaware.

A brief outline of the history of Syriac scholarship can be found in my "The development of Syriac studies", in K.J. Cathcart (ed.), *The Edward Hincks Bicentenary Lectures* (Dublin, 1994), pp. 94–113; and surveys of scholarship in my "Syriac Studies in the last three decades: some reflections", in R. Lavenant (ed.), *VI Symposium Syriacum 1992* (Orientalia Christiana Analecta 247; Rome, 1994), pp. 13–29, "A half century of Syriac studies", *Byzantine and Modern Greek Studies* 40 (2016), pp. 38–48, and "Developments in Syriac studies over half a century (1964–2014)", *The Harp* 31 (2016), pp. 1–15; also "The contribution of departed Syriacists, 1997–2006", *Hugoye* 10 (2007), pp. 7–22. For the wider topic of Oriens Christianus, see especially H. Kaufhold, "Die Wissenschaft vom christichen Orient. Gedanke zur Geschichte und Zukunft des Faches", in P. Bruns and H.O. Luthe (eds), *Vom Euphrat an die Altmühle* (Eichstätter Beiträge zur christlichen Orient 1; Wiesbaden, 2012), pp. 15–214; also on the future, L. van Rompay, "Syriac studies: the challenge of the coming decade", *Hugoye* 10 (2007), pp. 23–35, is still applicable.

EPILOGUE: THE DELIGHTS OF MANUSCRIPTS

To read, as one sits in the Oriental Studies Room of the British Library, the words "this volume was completed in the month Teshri II of the year 723 in Urhay, capital of Beth Nahrin" is a moving experience, for at the end of this, the earliest of all dated Syriac manuscripts (411 of the Christian era), is also a list of names of Persian martyrs, almost certainly brought back from Seleucia-Ktesiphon only a few months previously by Marutha, bishop of Martyropolis, who had been serving as ambassador to the Sasanid court. It does not take much imagination to find oneself transported back across time and space to Edessa in November 411. This moving experience was repeated when, in 2005, in the course of cataloguing, with Lucas van Rompay, the Syriac materials in the Library of Deir al-Surian, I suddenly recognized, on a diminutive fragment, the very distinctive small script of the same manuscript: indeed it turned out to be part of the torn final folio of the manuscript now in the British Library; equally moving was the discovery that this fragment contained the names of the women martyrs.

As a matter of fact the first Syriac manuscript I ever had the joy of handling was a rather scruffy and torn fragment on a visit to Beirut as an undergraduate; although it was no more than a couple of hundred years old at the most, my curiosity was aroused by the mention of the fifth century emperor Marcian. On return home I managed to identify the text as a fragment of the Life of the fierce monk Barsoma who successfully scared off his theological opponents at the second council of Ephesus in 449. The excitement caused me by this very minor discovery proved addictive, but fortunately for one's pocket one does not necessarily have to go to the Middle East to browse among Syriac manuscripts; London and Birmingham happen to possess two of the largest collections of Syriac manuscripts in the world. The bulk of those in the British Library are exceptionally old, some belonging to the fifth and sixth centuries—thanks to their having been preserved until the mid-nineteenth century in the Syrian monastery (Deir al-Surian, now Coptic Orthodox) the Nitrian desert, between Alexandria and Cairo. The manuscripts in the Mingana Collection of the Selly Oak Colleges Library, Birmingham, on the other hand, are mostly very recent (one was copied as late as 1932), but nevertheless they contain several works not otherwise represented in Western libraries. They were collected by Alphonse Mingana (whose name has figured earlier) during the course of two journeys to the Middle East financed by the generosity of Edward Cadbury.

Syriac scribes usually follow the old tradition, already found in ancient Mesopotamia, of adding at the end of the text they are copying a colophon, giving details of the date and place of writing, as well as their own name; and if there was empty space still available, their *horror vacui* might lead them to fill it with imprecations against anyone who borrowed the book and failed to return it. Jottings about some contemporary event might also find their way into empty end leaves, and one of the earliest accounts, and probably contemporary, of the Arab invasion of Palestine is to be found on the fly leaf of a sixth-century Gospel manuscript in the British Library. The scribe of a much more recent (late nineteenth-century) Mingana manuscript has left us with a moving narrative of several pages describing the massacre just suffered by the Syrian Orthodox communities of southeastern Turkey in 1895–96.

Habent sua fata libelli. Later owners, as well as the original scribes, were apt to add their names to manuscripts, sometimes even mentioning the price they paid for it. One such owner, to whom Syriac scholarship owes an inestimable debt, was Moses of Nisibis, abbot of Deir al-Surian. Shortly after 926 he went to Baghdad to petition the Caliph on the matter of the tax problems faced by his own and other Egyptian monasteries. Sorting out tax affairs was a slow business then, just as it often is now, and before he finally returned to his monastery in 932 he took the opportunity to visit various Mesopotamian monasteries, buying up old Syrian manuscripts wherever he could. In this way he accumulated a magnificent collection of texts—which today form the nucleus of both the Vatican and the British Library holdings of Syriac manuscripts (some of those in the Vatican, bought in the early eighteenth century, still bear the marks of a mishap on the journey to Rome, when a load of them fell into the Nile). An attempt to reconstruct the contents of Moses' superb library, on the basis of his various notes of ownership, was made by H. Evelyn White in his *The History of the Monasteries of Nitria and Scetis* (New York, 1923).

Although the authorities of the British Museum were led to believe that they had bought up from the monastery all remaining Syriac manuscripts that had been left by Elias Assemani in 1707, it is now known that several dozen old Syriac manuscripts still remain in the monastery;

these have now been described by Lucas van Rompay and myself in our *Catalogue of the Syriac Manuscripts and Fragments in the Library of Deir al-Surian, Wadi al-Natrun (Egypt)* (Orientalia Lovaniensia Analecta 227; Leuven, 2014), accompanied by over 300 pages of images of manuscripts.

Owners of manuscripts, both ancient and modern, sometimes like to obliterate any too telling evidence of a manuscript's origin. In the Mingana collection there is a group of single leaves of early manuscripts cut out with scissors from their rightful home, and in several cases it is possible to mate them up—at least figuratively—with the original manuscripts from which they were taken—all at St. Catharine's Monastery on Mount Sinai: one pair of leaves indeed proved to be part of a unique manuscript containing the works of the seventh-century mystic Sahdona (or Martyrius), the author of a very fine work on spirituality. Today this manuscript, not quite complete, is divided up between Birmingham, Strassbourg, St Petersburg, and Milan. The publication of Mother Philothea of Sinai's catalogue of the "New Finds" at the Monastery has happily revealed that part of the manuscript in fact still remains in the Monastery.[21] A word of warning: such chance discoveries of "marriages" between loose leaves in different libraries can have unexpected, and time-consuming consequences: one turned out to involve me in the writing of an entire book.[22] But this is part of the fascination of the whole business.

European and American libraries are usually reasonably well catalogued, but catalogues do not always give away the true nature of a manuscript's actual contents. I would never have looked at "Initium martyrii Maximi Palaestinensis" if I had not been interested in another text in the same manuscript, yet this turned out to be an astonishing document—an early "anti-life" of Maximus the Confessor (died 662), written by a theological opponent, evidently within a few decades of his death. According to this work, Maximus was born and educated in Palestine, and not Constantinople—which would nicely explain his friendship with Sophronius, patriarch of Jerusalem. The manuscript in

---

[21] Syriac M45N in Philothée du Sinaï, *Nouveaux manuscrits syriaques du Sinaï* (Athens, 2008), pp. 474–8. Small fragments, not covered in her catalogue, are described in my *Catalogue of Syriac Fragments (New Finds) in the Library of the Monastery of Saint Catherine, Mount Sinai* (Athens, 1995). A scholar who has done a great deal in recent years joining up prts of Sinai manuscripts which are now scattered all of the world is Paul Géhin, notably in a series of articles in *Oriens Christianus* 90, 91 and 94 (2006–7, 2010).

[22] *The Syriac Version of the Pseudo-Nonnos Mythological Scholia* (Cambridge, 1971).

question proved to be a very rare example of an early Maronite text, and it incidentally threw some light on the exceedingly obscure origins of the Maronites themselves.

In the case of Middle Eastern libraries, for which catalogues are a rarity, the unexpected is always present (provided one can get access in the first place!). What treasures are still to be found there can be seen from the lengthy list of Arthur Vööbus' discoveries as a result of his systematic examination of these collections (the bibliography of his publications, given in the recent *Festschrift* in his honour, runs to over 50 monographs and 200 articles!). Fortunately today, thanks to the work of the Hill Museum & Monastic Library (HMML) at St John's University, Collegeville, many of these Middle Eastern collection have been digitized and catalogued, thus making them immensely more accessible to scholars.

One exciting moment in my own experience was when I came across a note going back to the great twelfth-century Patriarch, Michael the Great, author of the largest and most important Syriac Chronicle. The note was to the effect that it was he who was behind the copying of the huge two-volume collection of Lives of the Saints which I had perched precariously on a diminutive coffee table in the office of the secretary to the Syrian Orthodox Patriarch in Damascus. (On a subsequent visit the Patriarch, His Holiness Mar Ignatius Yakub III, had very kindly allowed me to work in the library itself—almost an embarras de richesse!).

It is usually only in the larger episcopal libraries that really old manuscripts are now to be found, but almost every village church will have a small collection of liturgical manuscripts (for the most part printed books are not used in church services). The colophons of these can often prove to be an unexpected source for local history. An unusually long colophon in a *Fenqitho* (the approximate equivalent of a Western breviary) which I once saw at the Syrian Orthodox monastery of Mar Gabriel in Tur Abdin told how the manuscript had originally been written in 1838 by a novice called Zaytun at Mar Gabriel, then recently repopulated after it had lain desolate for 120 years as a result of various pillages. Probably in 1915, called "the year of the sword" in local tradition (because of the large-scale massacres), it had been taken as plunder by Muslims from the monastery, but eventually in 1929 it had been bought back by a certain sub-deacon George, who then donated it to the village church of Keferze (also in Tur ʿAbdin), where it had remained until some years ago, when the abbot of Mar Gabriel, Rabban Samuel Aktash (now Mar Timotheos, bishop of Tur ʿAbdin), together with the head of the monastic school there, Malfono Isa Gülten (Garis), happened to visit the church and read the colophon; they arranged to have another *Fenqitho* copied for the church, and so the manuscript of 1838 (a fine piece of calligraphy) has now been returned to its original home where it is greatly cherished.

As my experience with the Life of Maximus the Confessor had indicated, it is not always necessary to travel far in order to make an exciting discovery. One that was almost literally on my doorstep took place in the Bodleian Library in Oxford. Idly looking through a card index of uncatalogued manuscripts I noticed one containing works by the seventh-century monastic author, Isaac of Niniveh, whose works have come to be widely read in many European languages, thanks to a Greek translation made at the Monastery of St. Saba, near Jerusalem, in the late eighth or early ninth century. As the Bodleian manuscript was said to be an early one, I ordered it up—to discover that it was a further volume of his writings, of which the only other complete manuscript had been destroyed during the First World War. The interest of these new texts can be gauged from the fact that there have already been translations into English, French, Italian, Catalan, Russian, Romanian, and Arabic.

It will come as a surprise to many to learn that Syriac manuscripts are still being copied in the Middle East. Facilities for printing Syriac are rare, and the printing press, donated by Queen Victoria, which the previous Syrian Orthodox metropolitan of Mardin, Mar Yuhannon Dolabani (+ 1969), had used for publishing a Syriac periodical, ceased to be active after 1956. The scribes are normally deacons, priests, or monks; the late Father Butrus Ögünc, who was a priest to one of the émigré Syriac communities in Germany, whom I first met when he was schoolmaster in the small town of Midyat in Tur 'Abdin, had written some 100 manuscripts by the time he was thirty years old! At first all the various liturgical books (and several literary texts) published from the Monastery of St. Ephrem in the Netherlands in the 1970s and 1980s were reproduced from the beautiful handwriting of Mor Julius Çiçek (died 2005), the first Syrian Orthodox bishop in Europe. With the advent of the possibility of printing Syriac with the computer, this has of course now changed. There is, however, a nice example of continuity: at the end of many of the books published by Mor Julius using computer technology he has retained a colophon that he had previously used when copying manuscripts; this reads "As the sailor rejoices when his boat reaches harbour, so does the scribe when he writes the last line." This happens to be a very ancient and widespread colophon, for it is also found in both Greek and Latin manuscripts in the Middle Ages; the earliest example of its use, however, is in Syriac, in a manuscript dated AD

543, and this happens to antedate the earliest Greek use of it by over a century.

If one has the privilege of meeting people from the different communities of Syriac tradition, such as Mar Aprem, Mor Gregorios Ibrahim, Mor Julius Çiçek, Fr. Yusuf Habbi, Chorepiscopus Pierre Yousif, Fr. Jacob Thekeparampil, Dr. George Kiraz, and Malphono Abrohom Nouro, to mention only some of those whose names have come up in the course of this Introduction, one quickly becomes aware that to study Syriac is to study a tradition which is still very much alive.

For further reading. There are helpful contributions on different aspects of Syriac manuscripts and codicology by E. Balicka-Witakowska, A. Binggeli, P.-G. Borbone, F. Briquel-Chatonnet, A. Desreumaux, G. Kessel, A. Mengozzi, A. Schmidt, and W. Witakoswki in A. Bausi (ed.), *Comparative Oriental Manuscript Studies. An Introduction* (Hamburg, 2015). Some basic information can also be found in chapter 8, "The Art of the Scribe", in vol. II of *The Hidden Pearl* (for which, see Section H, at the end).

Appendix: The Syriac Churches

Syriac literature is closely tied to church history, and the variety of names in use for the various Syriac churches, coupled with the popular misconceptions which are current (even in otherwise reliable modern works) about their theological position, combine to increase the bewilderment of the outsider and the newcomer to the subject.

First of all it will be helpful to clarify the confusing terminology by means of a table:

Official name	Also known as	Other sobriquets	Eastern Catholic counterpart (in communion with Rome)
Syrian Orthodox Church	West Syrian/c	Monophysite, Jacobite	Syrian Catholic Church
Church of the East (more recently "Assyrian Church of the East" and "Ancient Church of the East")	East Syrian/c	Nestorian, Assyrian	Chaldean Catholic Church

The terms "Nestorian" and "Monophysite" were originally devised as opprobrious epithets, and imply the holding of heretical opinions; as such they are misleading and should definitely be avoided. "Jacobite" derives from Jacob Baradaeus who reorganized the Syrian Orthodox Church in the mid-sixth century at a time when the emperor Justinian was trying to suppress its hierarchy. "Assyrian," very popular today in the Middle East and émigré communities (since for many it provides a much sought for "national" identity) seems to originate, as far as its present day connotations are concerned, with the conjecture of some nineteenth-century archaeologists and missionaries that the modern Christian population of northern Iraq are descendants of the ancient Assyrians.[23] This was taken up especially among people in the Church of the East. (One consequence of the adoption of an Assyrian identity has been the giving of names such as Sargon and Hammurabi to children). As it happens, "Assyrian" serves well alongside the term "Chaldean" which applies to that part of the Church of the East which first entered into union with Rome (in the mid-sixteenth century).

The need felt for a recognizable ethnic (as opposed to religious) designation arises above all in the large diaspora communities in Europe, the Americas, and Australia. For the Syrian Orthodox, the term "Syrian" has been usurped by the modern state of Syria, and for those who come from other Middle Eastern countries this is particularly problematic. Various alternatives have been adopted, including (by the more secular-minded) "Assyrian," which has caused considerable controversy (and trouble in some countries);[24] a better choice would seem to be "Aramaean." Another recent solution is to use "Syriac" as an ethnic term, as well as referring to the language and the literature. In the present Introduction I have used "East Syriac" and "West Syriac" as the most practical general designations.

The matter is in fact even more complicated by the fact that there are today eight different Churches which have a Syriac liturgical tradition (even if only a few of them actually still employ the language Syriac in their liturgy). At their roots, the divisions that exist today between the various Syriac (and other Eastern) Churches originate in the different stands taken over the christological controversies of the fifth century. Convenient touchstones are provided by the two main councils of that century: the Council of Ephesus in 431, and the Council of Chalcedon in 451. The mainstream of Christian tradition, represented today by the Eastern Orthodox Churches (Greek, Russian, etc.), the Maronite and other Eastern Rite Catholic Churches, the Roman Catholic Church together with the various derived Western reformed Churches, accept both Councils, whereas the Syrian Orthodox Church (along with the other Oriental Orthodox Churches, Armenian, Coptic, Ethiopic) accepts Ephesus but rejects the

---

[23] For the origins of the adoption of the name, there is a well-documented study by A.H. Becker, *Revival and Awakening. American Evangelical Missionaries in Iran and Iraq and the Origins of Assyrian Nationalist* (Chicago, 2015).

[24] There is an excellent article on this term by W. Heinrichs, 'The modern Assyrians—name and nation', in R. Contini and others (eds.), *Semitica. Serta Philologica C. Tsereteli dicata* (Turin, 1993), pp. 99–114.

definition of faith laid down at Chalcedon (which eventually became the official doctrine of the Roman Empire from the reign of Justin I (518–27) onwards). The Church of the East, situated outside the Roman Empire at the time of the Councils convened by the Roman Emperor, had no part in either, but disapproves of the Council of Ephesus and finds the Chalcedonian Definition of Faith illogical.

Looked at theologically, the Church of the East represents one end of the theological spectrum, making a distinction between the divine and human natures in the incarnate Christ (with the consequence that they do not give Mary the title of Theotokos, "bearer of God," but only Christotokos). The mainstream Christian also makes a distinction between the two natures, while the Syrian Orthodox (and other Oriental Orthodox) speak of see only one nature in the incarnate Christ, "composed" out of two: to them, the presence of any duality in the incarnate Christ would vitiate the full reality of the incarnation. Ironically the Chalcedonian definition of faith, which ended up by declaring that the incarnate Christ existed "*in* two natures," had in the text of its earlier draft "*out* of two natures"—a formula which is perfectly acceptable to the Oriental Orthodox Churches. Here it should be emphatically stressed that, contrary to widespread Western opinion, the Syrian Orthodox do *not* hold that the one nature in Christ is *only* the divine, having "swallowed up" the human: this is the Eutychian position, which the Syrian Orthodox have always condemned as completely heretical. Thus the term "Miaphysite", recently introducied, rather than "Monophysite," is a much more appropriate one by which to describe the Oriental Orthodox Churches, in contrast to the "Dyophysite" Churches which accept Chalcedon.[25]

In the course of the sixteenth to eighteenth centuries contact with the Roman Catholic Church led to the creation of separate Eastern Rite Catholic hierarchies, thus bringing into existence the Chaldean Catholic Church (in the mid-sixteenth century) and the Syrian Catholic Church in the seventeenth.

The following Table will help to illustrate the place of the various Syriac Churches within the Christian tradition as a whole (the Syriac Churches are indicated in bold):

---

[25] See the various contributions to *Cristianesimo nella Storia* 37 (2016) on the subject.

'two nature' christology (dyophysite)

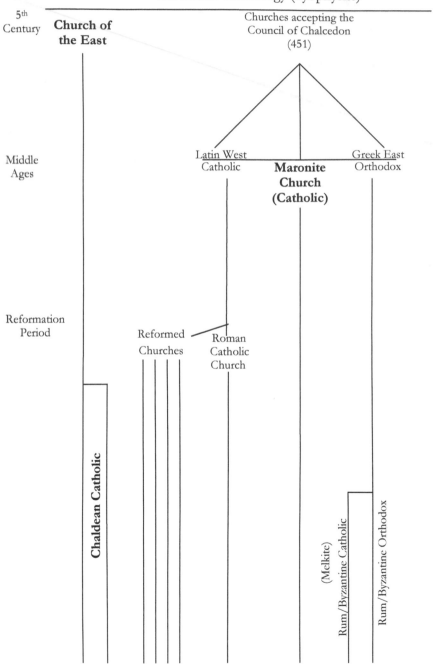

5th
Century

**Church of
the East**

Churches accepting the
Council of Chalcedon
(451)

Middle
Ages

Latin West
Catholic

**Maronite
Church
(Catholic)**

Greek East
Orthodox

Reformation
Period

Reformed
Churches

Roman
Catholic
Church

Chaldean Catholic

(Melkite)

Rum/Byzantine Catholic

Rum/Byzantine Orthodox

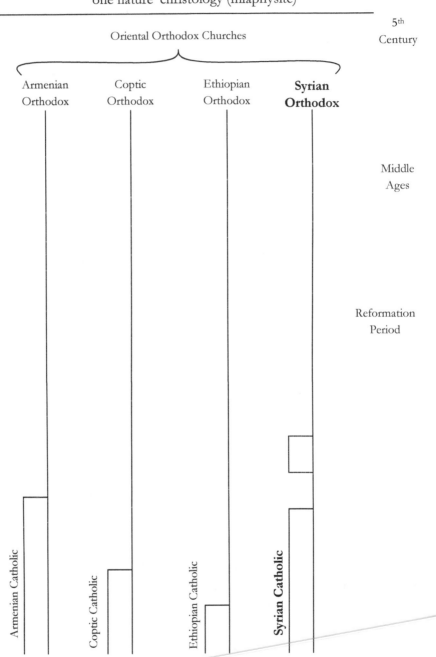

Christianity reached south India with St. Thomas, according to an early tradition. This is not inconceivable, and a Christian community was certainly establised there by an early date, its hierarchical links being with the Church of the East in Mesopotamia. Unfortunately very few historical records are available prior to the arrival of the Portuguese (first with Vasco da Gama in 1498). The misguided attempt to latinize the liturgical tradition led to fragmentation of the once single ecclesiastical tradition, and today there are no less than seven different Churches of Syriac liturgical tradition in India (mainly in the State of Kerala); these include the only Reformed Orthodox Church, the Mar Thoma Syrian Church.

The confusing situation presented by the various different Syriac Churches can best be set out diagrammatically. In the following Table 3 those names in italics refer to Churches of Syriac tradition in India; it will be noticed that, to add to the confusion, the term "Chaldean" denotes one thing in the Middle East, and quite another in India! Separate numbers indicate separate Churches.

West Syriac Liturgical Tradition			East Syriac Liturgical Tradition	
Orthodox	Reformed	Catholic	Catholic	Church of the East
1. Syrian Orthodox Church; *Malankara Syrian Orthodox Church*	*Mar Thoma Syrian Church*	1. Maronite Church	1. Chaldean Catholic Church	1. Assyrian Church of the East; *Chaldean Church*
2. *Malankara Orthodox Syrian Church*		2. Syrian Catholic Church	2. *Syro-Malabar Church*	2. Ancient Church of the East
3. *Malabar Independent Syrian Church*		3. *Malankara Catholic Church*		

A few words should be said about each of these Churches, which all belong to the Syriac cultural world.

THE WEST SYRIAC LITURGICAL TRADITION

The Syrian Orthodox Church only gradually became separated from the mainstream church in the course of the late fifth and the sixth century, and it was not until the first half of the sixth century that a separate hierarchy developed as a result of the deposition, by the emperor Justin, of the anti-Chalcedonian patriarch of Antioch, Severus. Since then their patriarch (one of five patriarchs of Antioch today) has never resided at Antioch; the present patriarch, His Holiness Mor Ignatius Aphram II resides in Damascus. Syrian Orthodox communities are now chiefly to be found in Syria, Lebanon, Turkey (Tur 'Abdin in the southeast, and Istanbul), Iraq, and India (Kerala); there are also very sizable émigré communities in Western Europe (Germany, the Netherlands, Sweden, and several other countries) and the Americas: the first Syrian Orthodox Archbishop of North America, Mor Athanasius Yeshue Samuel, was the first purchaser of the famous Isaiah scroll from Qumran; there is a fascinating account of this episode in his *Treasure of Qumran: My Story of the Dead Sea Scrolls* (London, 1968), though this should now be read in conjunction with George Kiraz (ed.), *Anton Kiraz's Archive on the Dead Sea Scrolls* (Piscataway NJ, 2005).

The Syrian Catholic Church, with its own Patriarch (in Beirut), has its origins in the late seventeenth century.

The twentieth century has witnessed two great scholar patriarchs, the Syrian Catholic Ephrem Rahmani (died 1929), and the Syrian Orthodox Ephrem (Afram) Barsoum (died 1957), the latter being the author of the important history of Syriac literature entitled *The Scattered Pearls*, mentioned earlier.

The presence of a West Syriac hierarchy and liturgical tradition in India goes back to the mid-seventeenth century and the reaction against the Portuguese policy of latinization. Both the Malankara Syrian Orthodox and Orthodox Syrian Churches now have their own Catholicos, the former being under the Patriarchate of Antioch; this sad schism goes back to the early twentieth century and attempts to heal it have unfortunately been short-lived. The Malabar Independent Syrian Church (a single diocese) goes back to 1774, while the reformed Mar Thoma Church came into existence at the end of the nineteenth century. The Malankara Catholic Church goes back to 1930, when Mar Ivanios and his flock entered into communion with Rome.

THE EAST SYRIAC LITURGICAL TRADITION

The Church of the East was from the first based outside the Roman Empire, and so its history has always been distinct from that of the other Churches, whose roots all lie within the Roman Empire. It is indicative of the poor communication between Christians in the two Empires that it was only in 410 that the Council of Nicaea (325) became known to, and was officially accepted by, the Church of the East. Whereas martyrdom was effectively brought to an end in the Roman Empire by the conversion of Constantine, it was only in the mid-fourth century that Persian Christians experienced their first serious bout of persecution from the Zoroastrian authorities. Persecution was to continue intermittently right up to the collapse of the Sasanid Empire in the seventh century; in many instances the martyrs were converts from Zoraoastianism who came from prominent families. A remarkable feature of the history of this Church is its missionary expansion across Asia, reaching China by 635—an event recorded on a bilingual Syriac-Chinese stele erected in 781, mentioned above.

Although European writers have derogatively called this Church "Nestorian," its connections with Nestorius are rather tenuous, and the term is definitely misleading since it means very different things to different people.[26] As a matter of fact, beside their own great theologian, Babai (died 628), the East Syrian Church's main source of theological inspiration was provided by the writings of the Greek Theodore of Mopsuestia (died 428), several of whose works survive complete only in Syriac translation.

During the last hundred years or so the history of this Church has been a particularly tragic one, and since 1972 there has been a schism: currently there are two patriarchs, one, Mar Dinkha IV (and from 2015, Mar Gewargis III Sliwa), of the Assyrian Church of the East (which follows the Gregorian, or New, Calendar), the other, Mar Addai II, of the Ancient Church of the East (which follows the Julian, or Old, Calendar). It so happened that the late patriarch, Mar Dinkha, was consecrated in England, in St. Barnabas' Church, Ealing (on October 17, 1976), but was resident in the United States, whereas Mar Addai is in Baghdad; Mar Gewargis, who had been Metropolitan of Baghdad, has remained in Iraq, based in Erbil. Their people are to be found in Syria, Lebanon, Iraq, Iran, and south India (Kerala), though today, with the large-scale emigration of Christians from the Middle East, there are probably many more living in America, Europe,

---

[26] See my "The 'Nestorian' Church: a lamentable misnomer," in J. F. Coakley and K. Parry (eds.), *The Church of the East. Life and Thought* (= Bulletin of the John Rylands University Library, Manchester, 78:3; 1996), pp. 22–35.

and Australia. This also applies to the vigorous Chaldean Catholic Church, whose Patriarch still resides in Iraq.

The Chaldean Church (in particular through the work of the late Fr. Yusuf Habbi) was the moving force behind the creation of Babel College in Baghdad (in 1991), which offered courses in Theology and Philosophy for the benefit of all the Christian communities in Iraq—a remarkable contribution to ecumenism in the field of theological education; alas, however, recent events have brough all this to an end. Among the cultural publications of the Chaldean Church, the periodical *Bayn al-Nahrayn* ("Mesopotamia") has many acticles of academic interest for Syriac studies. In recent years there have been important moves aimed at bringing the Chaldean Catholic Church and the Assyrian Church of the East together.

Needless to say, the Gulf War of 1990 and the invasion of Iraq in 2003 have had a disastrous effect on all the Christian communities in that country, causing massive emigration as well as destruction.

THE MARONITE CHURCH

The origins of the Maronites as a separate church are obscure, although they are evidently tied up somehow with the monothelete/dyothelete controversy of the seventh and early eighth century. The Maronite Church has accepted the authority of Rome since the time of the Crusades and their Patriarch Jeremiah II assisted at the Fourth Lateran Council in 1215. The Maronite Patriarch (one of the five Patriarchs of Antioch) now resides outside Beirut; over the last century or so, in particular, the Maronite patriarchate has played an important role in Lebanese politics.

At Kaslik, just south of Jounieh in the Lebanon, there is a Maronite university run by the Order of Lebanese Monks, the Université Saint-Esprit, which produces the excellent periodical *Parole de l'Orient*, mentioned earlier. Another monastic order, that of the Antonines, is also active in promoting a better knowledge of the Syriac heritage, and their Centre d'études et de recherches orientales (CERO), at Antelias, has organised the annual colloquia on the "Patrimoine syriaque," also mentioned earlier.

As has already been seen, the Maronites played an important role in the history of Syriac scholarship in Europe ever since the establishment in Rome of the Maronite College (in 1584). In the seventeenth century it was a Maronite, Gabriel Sionita, who was largely responsible for the Syriac text in the great Paris Polyglot Bible, while in the eighteenth century the Assemani family produced a notable succession of Syriac scholars, chief among whom was Joseph Simon Assemani (+ 1768): his *Bibliotheca Orientalis*, a survey of Syriac literature based on the riches of the Vatican Library (Rome, 1719–

28), has already been mentioned as still being a basic resource for Syriac studies.

THE BYZANTINE (RUM) ORTHODOX PATRIARCHATE OF ANTIOCH

Besides the Syrian Orthodox, Syrian Catholic, and Maronite Patriarchs of Antioch, there are two further ones, both belonging to the Chalcedonian tradition, the Byzantine (Rum) Orthodox and Melkite Catholic. The Chalcedonian Patriarchate of Antioch historically belongs to the Churches which have a Syriac heritage, for one of its literary and liturgical languages was once Syriac: Syriac, however, was replaced as a literary language by Arabic from the ninth century onwards, though it continued in use as a liturgical language in certain areas until as late as the seventeenth century. Furthermore, its liturgical tradition was once Antiochene (and thus closely related to the Syrian Orthodox and Maronite traditions), but in about the tenth and eleventh centuries (when part of north Syria was termporarily reconconquered by the Byzantine Empire), its rite was completely adapted to that of Constantinople.

The term "Melkite" is regularly used when speaking of Syriac manuscripts belonging to this tradition, but it should be noted that when "Melkite" is used as an ecclesiastical term it refers specifically to the Eastern Rite Catholic Patriarchate of Antioch (which came into existence in the eighteenth century), and not to the Orthodox one.

ECUMENICAL DIALOGUE

All the different Syriac Churches are now involved in ecumenical dialogue. Particularly important events have been the joint declarations of faith made by the Syrian Orthodox Patriarch, Ignatius Zakka I and Pope John Paul II in 1984, and by the Patriarch of the Assyrian Church of the East, Dinkha IV, and Pope John Paul II in 1994. It was also in the year 1994 that the PRO ORIENTE Foundation in Vienna initiated its series of "Syriac Dialogue," involving all the different Churches of Syriac tradition, Chalcedonian, Oriental Orthodox, and Church of the East. The papers produced for these meetings are published under the title *Syriac Dialogue* (1, 1994; 2, 1996; 3, 1998; 4, 2001; 5, 2003; 6, 2004).

SOME LITERATURE

A general historical survey of all the various oriental churches is given in A. S. Atiya, *A History of Eastern Christianity* (London, 1968). For the modern period both D. Attwater's *The Christian Churches of the East* (2 volumes; London, 1968), which gives information on ecclesiastical matters, and R. B. Betts' *Christians in the Arab East* (London, 1979), which is concerned more with demography and politics, are still useful. A listing of the current hierarchy of all the Syriac Churches is given by J. Madey, *The Hierarch of the Churches of East and West Syriac Traditions* (Moran Etho 17; Kottayam, 2002).

Helpful introductory works on the individual Syriac Churches today include the following:

Syrian Orthodox and Syrian Catholic:

- S. P. Brock, with D.G.K. Taylor (eds.), *The Hidden Pearl*, III. *At the Turn of the Third Millennium: the Syrian Orthodox Witness* (Rome, 2001). [For the contents, see above, at the end of Ch.V H].

- C. Chaillot, *The Syrian Orthodox Church of Antioch and all the East. A Brief Introduction to its Life and Spirituality* (Geneva, 1998). This delightful personal account provides a lot of information that is not readily available elsewhere.

- C. Sélis, *Les syriens orthodoxes et catholiques* (Turnhout, 1988).

- M. Tamcke, *Die Christen vom Tur Abdin. Hinführung zur Syrische-Orthodoxen Kirche* (Frankfurt am Main, 2009).

Church of the East and Chaldean Church:

- Mar Aprem, *The Assyrian Church of the East in the Twentieth Century* (Kottayam, 2003).

- W. Baum and D. Winkler, *The Apostolic Church of the East* (London 2003), ch. 5.

- C. Baumer, *The Church of the East. An Illustrated History of Assyrian Christianity* (London, 2006).

- J. F. Coakley and K. Parry (eds.), *The Church of the East, Life and Thought* (= Bulletin of the John Rylands University Library, Manchester, 78:3, 1996).

- A. O'Mahony, "Eastern Christianity in Modern Iraq," in A. O'Mahony (ed.), *Eastern Christianity. Studies in Modern History, Religion and Politics* (London, 2004), pp. 11–43.

- S. Rassam, *Christianity in Iraq* (Leominster, 2005).

- H. Teule, *Les Assyro-Chaldéens. Chrétiens d'Iraq, d'Iran et de Turquie* (Turnhout, 2008). An excellent general introduction.

The Maronite Church:

- P. Dib, *History of the Maronite Church* (Detroit, 1971).

- J. Mahfouz, *Short History of the Maronite Church* (Jounieh, 1987).

- R. Mouawad, *Les Maronites* (Turnhout, 2009). An excellent general introduction.

- Much information can be found in A. J. Salim's *Captivated by Your Teachings. A Resource Book for Adult Maronite Catholics* (Tucson, 2002).

The Chalcedonian Patriarchates of Antioch, Orthodox and Catholic:

- I. Dick, *Les Melkites. Grec-orthodoxes et grec-catholiques des patriarcats d'Antioche, d'Alexandrie et de Jérusalem* (Turnhout, 1994). English translation 2004.

Middle Eastern Christianity in general
See especially the various contributions to A. O'Mahony (ed.), *Eastern Christianity: Studies in Modern History, Religion and Politics* (London, 2004), and *Christianity in the Middle East. Studies in Modern History, Theology and Politics* (London, 2008); and A. O'Mahony and E. Loosley (eds), *Eastern Christianity in the Modern Middle East* (London, 2010).

India:

- L. W. Brown, *The Indian Christians of St Thomas* (2nd ed., Cambridge, 1982).

- C. Chaillot, *The Malankara Orthodox Church* (Geneva, 1996).

- D. Daniel, *The Orthodox Church of India. A History* (2nd ed. New Delhi, 1986).

- E. Tisserant, *Eastern Christianity in India* (London, 1957).

Among the many late nineteenth- and early twentieth-century works, a particularly fascinating account of the Syrian Orthodox Church at the end of the nineteenth century is given by O. H. Parry, *Six Months in a Syrian Monastery* (London, 1895)—the monastery was Deir ez Zafaran, on the edge of Tur ʿAbdin in southeastern Turkey; at that time it was the seat of the patriarch. Thanks to the Anglican educational missions to the Church of the East there are several readable accounts of this Church and its people, notably A. J. Maclean and W. H. Browne, *The Catholicos of the East and his People* (London, 1892), and W. A. Wigram, *The Assyrians and their Neighbours* (London, 1929). The older work by G. P. Badger, *The Nestorians and their Rituals* (two volumes; London, 1852) has become something of a classic.

An outline of ecumenical developments involving the Syriac Churches can be found in my "The Syriac Churches in ecumenical dialogue on christology," in A. O'Mahony (ed.), *Eastern Christianity. Studies on Modern History, Religion and Politics* (London, 2004), pp. 44–65, and "The Syriac Churches of the Middle East and Dialogue with the Catholic Church", in A. O'Mahony and J. Flannery (eds), *The Catholic Church in the Contemporary Middle East* (London, 2010), pp. 107–18. Regular updates on dialogue can be found in the journal *Proche Orient Chrétien*. For Oriental-Eastern Orthodox Dialogue, see the contributions by Mor Polycarpus Aydin and B. Varghese in C. Chaillot (ed.), *The Dialogue between the Eastern Orthodox and Oriental Orthodox Churches* (Volos, Greece, 2016).